Contextual Issues

Theological, Ethical and Missiological Responses

By the Same Author :

—Human Rights : Concepts and Perspectives
—Christian Ethics : Issues and Insights

About the Author

Rev.Dr.M.Stephen obtained degrees of B.A. and M.A. from Kerala University, B.D. and M. Th. from Serampore University followed by doctoral degree in. Theology awarded to him by Dharmaram Vidyashetram : Pontifical Alhonaeum of Philosophy and Theology, Bangalore. Presently he is Serving Faith Theological Seminary, Manakala, Adoor, Kerala as a theological teacher. He is a renowned writer and orator having authored several books and published numerous articles in English as well as Malayalam.

Contextual Issues

Theological, Ethical and Missiological Responses

Dr. M. Stephen

CONCEPT PUBLISHING COMPANY PVT. LTD.
NEW DELHI-110059

ISBN-13: 978-81-8069-769-2

First Published 2011

Published and Printed by

Concept
Since 1974

Concept Publishing Company Pvt. Ltd.
Regd. Office:
A/15-16, Commercial Block, Mohan Garden,
New Delhi-110059 (India)
Phones : 25351460, 25351794, *Fax* : 091-11-25357109
Email : publishing@conceptpub.com
Website: www.conceptpub.com

Editorial Office:
H-13, Bali Nagar, New Delhi-110 015, India

Cataloging in Publication Data--*Courtesy*: D.K. Agencies (P) Ltd. <docinfo@dkagencies.com>

Sttīphan, Em.
Contextual issues : theological, ethical and missiological responses / M. Stephen.
p. cm.
Includes index.
ISBN 9788180697692

1. Social problems. 2. Social problems--India. 3. Situation ethics. 4. Situation ethics-India. 5. Church and social problems. 6. Church and social problems--India. I. Title.

DDC 361.1 22

Introduction

In the context of today we are confronting several issues which are socio-economic, political and religious in nature.The contextual issues are the issues of the victimized or the marginalized as they undergo several kinds of oppressions. In a world of greed, selfishness, competition and exploitation, the injustices are at the increase which dehumanize many people. It is important to have missiological and ethical response to these issues. Missiology and Ethics are concerned of the contextual issues and these disciplines make responses to the issues in order to resolve them. Both these disciplines are analytical, reflective and liberative in nature.

Our context is having a number of issues which are to be responded from Christian point of view. There is a psycho-social element also in certain issues so it is inevitable to have an integration of theology, ethics, missiology and psychology in the process of making responses. I hope, this book 'Contextual Issues' can be an eye-opener to some of the realities around us,which can help us to respond creatively to them.

Rev.Dr. M. Stephen
Puthenparambil
Near Railway Station
Kottayam - 686001
Kerala, India.

Contents

I

God and Globalization

Introduction

The term "globalization" was first word by Theodore Levitt in 1985. The world becomes a global village. The commodities and informations are available everywhere as there is free-market. Joseph Stiglitz, the Nobel Prize Winner for Economics (2001) describes the benefits of globalization as follows :"International trade helps economic development when a country's exports drive its economic growth. Export-led growth was the counterpiece of the industrial policy that enriched much of Asia and left millions of people there far better off. Because of globalization many people in the world now live longer than before and their standard of living is far better" *(Globalization and its Discontents,* New Delhi, Penguin Books, 2002. P. 4). He continued to state, "Globalization has reduced the sense of isolation felt in much of the developing world and has given many people in the developing countries access to knowldge well beyond the reach of even the wealthiest in any country a century ago" (*Ibid.,* P. 4). Stiglitz does not see the neo-colonial elements in globalization which is very capital-intensive, exploitative and oppressive. It is also rooted in the Western hegemony over the poor. The control of the powerful over the product and resources which create the inequality and making the gulf between rich and poor is not quite noticed by him. Using deceptive methods and power by MNCS and TNCS to tap the resources of the Third World by collaborating with the Third World elites is also ignored by Stiglitz.

The Framework of Globalization

The IMF, World Bank and WTO (World Trade Organization) also have played key roles in the context of globalization. The International Monetary Fund and World Bank furnish money to the Third World development (eg. infrastructure) with a certain amount of interest and demanded the Government authorities to increase the taxes and take away the subsidy on food, water, electricity and fertilizers. This is to make people's life miserable, especially to the poor. World Trade Organization (Former GATT)control the field of agriculture. The genetic termination of seeds and the deceptive patent laws are made in order to create a dependence on them by Asian farmers and others. Globalization is rooted in the greed of the Western elites and not concerned of the need of the poor.

Transnationalization of capital, internationalization of labour, homogenization of culture, globalization of production, consumerism and affluence are the main focus of globalization which is a Western agenda, and they are not the concerns of the Third World people as they look forward for food, shelter, employment, a piece of land which are the means of survival. Globalization is not considering the basic needs of the people but the sovereignty of the market. Globalization is the ideology of the powerful who manipulate technology, wealth and trade for their selfish interests.

It is privatization and liberalization which are good for the capitalists than the people who are powerless and down-trodden which includes poor, black, victimized women, dalits and tribals. The forces of globalization marginalize them as they use their capacities and gather their resources in cheap rate. The cheap labour policy and grabbing the raw materials in low price are the examples for this. Globalization is a global phenomenon. It is a Western neo-colonial idea to control the whole world or to bring the Third World under their control. It is the old wine in new wineskins. It is the new form of exploitation such as feudalism or capitalism. It is promoted by the liberalization. The World Trade Organization (WTO) is playing a dominant role to insist it all over the world. The World Bank, International Monetary Fund, Multi-National Corporations and Transnational Corporations are taking lead to speed up the process of globalization.

Globalization presents a new market culture. It is consumeristic. It is based on free-market economy. The Western elites and multi-nationals collaborate with the elites of the Third World to systematically exploit the resources of the Third World. By making the market free, the goods are dumped into the market by the Western capitalistic force for the Third World people to buy it. They inspire the people to buy the luxury items, through advertisement. The indigenous goods and the Third World farmers are reaping the consequence of this globalization. In the competition the Indian goods fail to find market. The foreign goods may be also cheap compared to Indian goods as the multi-nationals have always mega-production and in the Third World market their products may find consideration for taxes because of some adjustments.

The forces of globalization brainwash the people through media. Though our indigenous drinks are cheaper and better, we are forced to buy the drinks such as coca cola or pepsi cola. By the use of media, these companies present it as an ideal, so it becomes a status symbol. Though some of the electronic goods are necessary, they present it as if no one can survive without these goods. They also suggest the ways in which one can buy these, though there is no money with him/her. Most of the companies are associated to the financial companies who would 'help' one to finance. They use all means to channelize the resources according to their interests. Make everyone slave of the market is the method of oppression advocated by globalization.

Globalization is introduced by the dominant for the

dominant. The poor are unnoticed in the Indian market, so also the farmers. The Indian products are not getting the deserved value as same products are importing from other countries. Most of the Indian producers who are indigenous in nature (not collaborating with West) are under going severe crisis. The poor are not having purchasing power, so they are rejected by the global market. The condition of the poor are pathetic, and the globalization does not provide upward mobility to them. Amirtya Sen said, unless there is a safety net for the poor, globalization is disastrous.

The globalization advocates "free market" is a neo-liberal ideology which is regulated by the First World. International banks and global monopolies are controlling the economy. The IMF and World Bank insist on Structural Adjustment Programme (SAP) which, according to Michel Chossudovsky, a form of "economic genocide." According to him, "This new form of economic and political domination – a form of "market colonialism " – subordinates people and Governments through the seemingly "neutral" interplay of market forces" *(The globalization of poverty,* New Delhi : Madhyam Book, 1997. P. 37). In his view, the execution of this global economic design has affected the livelihood of more than 80 per cent of the World population *(Ibid., P. 37).*

The consumeristic culture (eg. the luxury and entertainment – including sexual) are globally transported through media and other means and it challenges the traditional cultural values. The food (eg. kentuky fried chicken, coca-cola, pepsi, pizzahut and MacDonald) also plays a significant role in consumer culture as they promote the consumerism. Many people, especially the youths are attracted by the advertisement of this consumeristic enterprises. International promotion of their food items is a neo-colonial policy to tap our resources and to destroy our traditional food items and habits. A pineapple or mango juice is cheap and better than pepsi or coca-cola.

The globalization promotes competition, and efficiency and use their power and money and insist their dominance on the poor and powerless. The exclusive claim as in fundamentalism is found in the claim of the superiority over their products. Intellectual property right is one of the subtle means by which they impose their power on Third World countries. In fact, the global investors are hijacking our economy, agriculture, industry and culture. These are affecting the women, dalits and tribals as they are powerless and victimized. When the resources are tapped, the cheap labour policy is insisted, the agricultural and industrial sector are hijacked, the marginated groups are much affected compared to the elites. The means of survival of the marginated groups will be lost. The absolute control of few (capitalist) over the resources will globalize poverty. Globalization is the deceptive strategy of a mafia in order to control the structure and to exploit and accumulate wealth.

Christian Response to Globalization

Bible stands against any capital intensive or feudal and colonial or neo-colonial forces. Bible protests any exploitative and unjust structures. Bible is people - friendly and especially poor- friendly (Ex. 20: 21 - 22; Isa. 1: 15 - 17; Jere. 7: 11; Am. 2: 6 -7; 5:10 -12; 5: 24). The feudal structure in the prophetic time is equal to the spirit of globalization today, as both these structures are to exploit, oppress and manipulate the poor to accumulate wealth. In the case of Naboth, Ahab was using his power to acquire his property. He was oppressed in an inhuman way, as he was killed by Ahab to annexe his inheritance, which was vindicated by God (1Kg. Chapters 21 and 22).

God is just and righteous and he will not support the forceful evacuation of the poor in order to acquire their land. When Naboth resisted, he was evacuated by killing him to grab his vineyard as in the case of the poor, dalits and tribals in India. The Incarnation of Jesus is to save or to liberate the victimized (LK. 4: 16 - 21) and not to oppress the poor. Jesus was identifying with the poor and restored them. His coming was not to show his power, but to liberate the suffering and marginalized.

The evil systems are resisted by Jesus and prophets. Bible never endorses the oppressive structure. The consumerism, competition and manipulation are the inhuman policies which are hated by the Bible. Bible looks forward a humane society where everyone's welfare is taken care of. It also advocates the dignity and rights of the poor.

Any programme that is introduced should cater to the needs of the poor and also to uplift them. If the welfare of the poor is not taken into account, any system is disastrous. The present form of globalization is not at all aiming at the liberation of the poor, instead it is to help the rich to accumulate more wealth. The Bible is against any economic system which facilitate margination. Bible is for the liberation of the poor. It sides the poor and their cause. So the unjust economic system like the globalization has to be challenged. Jesus was siding with the poor and he vehemently criticized the explotiative economic structure which is controlled by the Roman and Jewish (rich class) nexus. The Globalization of poor is what is taking place now. So the Church has to awaken the conscience of the World to make aware of the dangers of globalization. Church also has to organize people to challenge the advocates of globalization.

2

The Major Ecological Issues

The term 'ecology' has come from the two Greek words 'oikos' and 'logos'. Oikos means the whole inhabited world, so ecology is a study on the environment and eco-systems of the whole world. The capitalistic tendencies and modernization in the form of industrialization and development and the consumeristic culture which are rooted in the sin of greed resulted in the disruption of harmony of the creation.

The major causes of ecological crisis

The sound that comes from vehicles, machineries and sound equipment, the emission of chemical waste, carbon dioxide, sulphur dioxide, carbon monoxide, chloro-fluro-oxides from factories and vehicle, deforestation and filling of agricultural lands in the name of development and the reckless use of pesticides have adversely affected the whole of creation. The generators emit the carbon-monoxide, the air-conditioners and the refrigerators emit the carbon fluro-oxides.

These have caused to different pollution such as air, sound and soil pollution, global warming, depletion of resources (the bio-diversity is affected, many species are in the verge of extinction and there is scarcity of water. The metals, minerals and fuel like petrol are also going to exhaust) and also to global climatic changes.

The war situation is also polluting the enviornment as the chemical and nuclear weapons are used in the warfare. The human greed and the spirit of colonialism or accumulation have led to this deep ecological crisis. The increased concentration of green houses like water vapour which effected 36-70 per cent. Carbon dioxide has effected 9-26 per cent, methane causes 4-9 per cent and troposperic ozone which causes 3-7 per cent of the greenhouse effect. Volcanic eruptions and solar variations also can cause the global warming and climate changes. It is observed, "water vapour also contributes to the natural greenhouse effect. As ocean temperature increase with global warming, evaporation over the oceans is expected to increase constituting a significant feedback that could further accelerate climate change" (*Global warming,* edited by K. C. Abraham, William Stanley *et. al.* Bangalore: SATHRI, 1994. P. 11).

The Effects or Consequences of Ecological Crises

The ecological crises have effected the creation in different ways. The earth is on a degeneration. Our every irresponsibility causes or effect on ecology.

1. *Global Warming/Global Climate Change*

The temperature of globe is going high. The ozone layer is damaged so there is radiation, especially the ultra-violet rays. The surface air temperature has increased by 0. 3 to 0. 6^0 celsius over the past hundred years (*Ibid.,* P. 13). The Inter-Governmental Panel on Climatic Change (IPCC) predicts on the severe effect on eco-systems. The consequences are as follows:

(a) Planetary climate changes will make weather patterns erratic and increasingly hard to predict.

Drought, storms, floods and hurricanes are likely to be more frequent and more severe than in the past. Ice, snow and glaciers will be reduced.

(b) As atmospheric warming increases the temperature of the ocean, it will expand and lead to a rise in sea level. A 30-50 centimetre (cm) increase in the level of the oceans is projected for 2050; it may reach between 65cm and 1 meter by the end of the 21st century. Coral reefs and other aquatic system will be disrupted.

(c) Effects on agriculture, due principally to changes in rainfall patterns and predictability, will be uneven but substantial. Some major cropland areas are likely to be lost, and others may be opened up. Desertification will be enhanced. Hydrological changes will be disruptive not only for agriculture but for hydroelectric power generation.

(d) Changed climate conditions will place stress on forests, grasslands and other ecosystems, especially where species are already close to their biological limit with respect to moisture and temperature. Forest losses, with the accompanying loss of wildlife habitats, will come on top of the alarming deforestation and species extinction already taking place.

(e) It is probable that the worst impact will be felt in economically weak societies. Small island states and low-lying coastal zones will be particularly vulnerable. Generally speaking the people in the South will be the first victims. In the words of the Second World Climate Conference, "In many cases the impacts will be felt most severely in regions already under

> stress, mainly in developing countries". Whatever their extent, the effects of accelerated climate change will exacerbate social inequalities within and between countries. (*Ibid.*, PP-13-14)

The effects can include the rise of sea level, retreat of glaciers and it is predicted that certain islands and places like Manhatten, Miami (both in USA) and Bangladesh will go under water. The space of the earth will be considerably reduced. A recent study also reveals that the climatic change has jeopardised the survival of the nation, which could be inaundated by water. It could also endanger the right to housing due to the scarcity of land ("climate change threatens Maldives" *The Hindu* (February 28, 2009 P. 18). The change in seasonal weather patterns effect the agriculture and also the economic system.

The climatic change can badly effect the ecosystems. The birds, animals and plants will be effected. The global warming can lead to their possible extinction. The increased radiation, heat and the unstable ecosystem will distrub the biotic life and their survival is in a threat. They may even vanish within no time.

2. *The threat to bio-diversity*

The ecological crises have effected badly the bio-diversity. The biotic life is suffered because of deforestation, depletion of resources, global warming pollutions and climate change. Deforestation will effect the wildlife and also the climate. The mega development projects will lead to deforestation which also badly effect the ecosystem and the bio-diversity. The plants, animals and birds and other organisms have lost their habitat. The pollution of water also does harm the water plants and creatures and also to humanity. The disturbance to habitat, it is observed, is effecting 60 per cent of birds and 70 per cent of animals (R. L. Sarkar, *The Bible, Ecology and Environment,* Delhi: ISPCK, 2000. P. 212). It is noted "Examination of the survival prospects of all forms of plant and animal life – including obscure ferns, shrubs, insects, mollusks, as well as elephants and wolves – indicates that huge numbers, of them have little future. Not hundreds, but hundreds of thousands of unique, irreplaceable life forms may vanish by the century's end" (*Ibid.,* P. 211). It is observed that more than a million species may have vanished within a short span of time. The habitat destruction is one of the main reasons for this tragedy (*Cry for Life,* edited by K. C. Abraham, Bangalore: SCM, 1993. P. 37).

According to K. Rajaratnam, "development tends to simplify ecosystems and to reduce their diversity of species. And species, once extinct, are not renewable. The loss of plant and animal species can greatly limit the options of future generations; so sustainable development requires the conservation of plant and animal species" (*Ecology and Development,* edited by Danel D. Chetti, Madras : UELCI, GLTCR & BTESSC, 199. P. 2). The deforestation and dessertification is going on in a rapid speed to destruct the ecosystem. It is found that each year between 11 and 15 million hectares of tropical forest are lost and every year six million hectares of land are irretrievably lost to dessertification (*Cry for Life;* P. 37).

3. *The different pollutions*

The pollutions are of different sort which affect the soil, water and air. The emission of toxic elements from the factories, automobiles and other unhygienic situation is hazardous to the health and survival of animals, birds, plants and human beings.

More than 2 billion people have inadequate drinking water and because of dirty water 25,000 people die in Third

World per day. They die of water-borne diseases. The water-borne diseases spawned by human wastes cause 80 per cent of all child births in the Third World. It is also reported that 10 per cent of all rivers may be described as heavily polluted (*Cry for Life*, PP. 36 -37).

According to R. L. Sarkar, "pollutants strair ecosystems and may reduce or eliminate population of sensitive species. Soil microbes have also suffered from pollution as industry sheds heavy metals and irrigated agriculture brings on salinization. Acid rain has made thousands of Scandinavian and North American lakes and pools virtually lifeless, and in combination with other kinds of air pollution, has damaged forests throughout Europe" (*The Bible, ecology* and *environment*, PP. 228- 229). The marine pollution, he observes, has defiled the mediterranean and other seas throughout the World. Air pollution has caused the global warming and the diseases like Asthma, Cancer, Bronchaic diseases and alleregic manifestations. The sound pollution can cause the hearing impairment and psychological disturbances. The soil can be spoiled because of fertilizers pesticides and dumping of wastes.

Acid rain is caused by the emission of sulphur and nitrogen (waste gases)which combine with water vapour, sunlight and oxygen are we transformed into weak acid droplets which fall into earth as dry particles or as rain or snow (*Ibid.*, P. 236). It is reported that 2/3 of the farmers in Brazil have suffered acute poisoning from pesticide. In China, the people live in cities are likely to die of lung cancer. As a result of rapid industrial and population growth in India, 70 per cent of surface water is polluted. In Malaysia most of the rivers are biologically and agriculturally dead due to industrial and agricultural waste. Ozone depletion causing skin cancer kills 1200 people every year in USA (*Ibid.*, P. 237). The Multinational and Transnational Corporations (MNCs and TNCs) have created a panic situation as they emit a large amount of toxic elements to pollute our ecosystem. The Chizo plastic company in Japan has channelled the waste (mercury) to minamatha sea gulf. This toxic element has killed the sea creatures and thousands of human beings in 1950s. The Union Carbide factory in Bhopal (India) in 1984 December 3 had the leakage of methyl and this pesticide company had killed (Bhopal tragedy)more than two thousand people and many are affected, and later it is reported that among the affected people between 1,000 and 10,000 may have died. Pesticides like DDT and Endosulfan are very poisonous as they can affect the health of people for generations and can make people disabled. The cities are also affected by smog which is a large scale outdoor pollution of automobile exhaust and industrial emissions.

The recent Copenhagen Summit (December 2009) was intended to reduce the emission of carbon in accordance with the Kyoto Protocol (December 1997). But this Summit was failure as the developed countries were not willing to reduce the emission on carbon. It is to be noted that USA which has only 4 per cent of World population emits 30 per cent of all green house gas emissions. The rich nations were working against in order that they could get away from the Kyoto Protocol.

4. *Depletion of resources/water scarcity*

The resources are depleted in a systematic way. The rain forests are lost at the rate of one football field a second. There is also extinction of flora and fauna. The animals, birds and plants including the aquatic ones are being wiped out from the face of the earth. R. L. Sarkar states, "Numerous forests, fisheries and wildlife resources have been over exploited, sometimes to the point of extinction. Historically, both the great auck and the passenger pigeon have succumbed to such pressure, and the Lebanon cedar that once blanketted 500,000 hectares now is found in only a few scattered remnants of forests". (R. L. Sarkar *OP. Cit;* P. 228). Sarkar states 'Ninety- eight per cent of the tropical dry forest along Central America's pacific coast has disappeared; it is observed' (R. L. Sarkar, *OP. Cit*; P. 228). Forests are the significant factor to regulate climate which is being wiped away at the rate of an acre per second which affected the habitat of the animals, birds and plants.

The modern industrial and economic activities are tapping the resources without any responsibility. The non-renewable energy like fossil fuels, minerals, the marine wealth and even water are tapped as part of our commerce and consumerism which affect the present and future generation. The whale and seals are being killed by hunters for commercial purposes are facing threat to survival. Ozone layer is needed for the existence of life on earth which is damaged and undergoing depletion. The rainforests are lost.

Besides the depletion of aquatic resources, the minerals, fuel and forest, a major ecological problem is the scarcity of water. The water deposit is contaminated, including the groundwater. The chemical and nuclear waste, the fertilizers, pesticides, and human waste have polluted the water. Lack of drinking water and proper sanitation leads to the death of around 4000 children every day. Two billion people live in the driest areas of the World.

The water use is also at the increases because of urbanization and industrialization. It is said that the next World War would be on the issue of water. People stand in que for water for many hours in Indian villages and other Third World countries. The traditional water deposits such as wells, ponds and rivers are dried up. Now, there is a heavy dependence on ground water, and it will also exhaust. The glaciers are shrinked so it is a threat to supply of water. By 2020 the water deposit will be reduced to 20-30 per cent.

A Christian Response to Ecological Problems

The principle of stewardship, conservation and preservation are important in Christian response to ecological crisis. Our attitudes, behaviour and actions are to be eco-friendly. The irresponsible use of resources and exploitation of resource are a consumeristic and capitalistic tendency which is to be curbed. If we love God, all creatures and love our neighbour (Mt 22: 36-37) we will love, care and support the creation, the creatures and resources in it. Concern for others, especially for the future generations is also a significant factor in an ethical and theological response. The ethics of care, that is rooted in stewardship upholds maintaining and protecting the trees, forests, the birds, animals, the aquatic creatures and other micro-organism, the minerals and water.

The only decision we have to make is whether we have to protect the creation or to destroy the creation? Genesis 1:28 does not indicate to torture the creation but to care the creation as a shepherd taken care of the sheep. There is no dominion over creation, but to protect the creation. The capitalistic, industrial, commercial and consumeristic forces are exploiting and misusing the resources and behaving irresponsibly to contribute to global warming so also to air, water sound and soil pollution and depletion of resources. The whole world is created by God and we are not supposed to spoil the creation (Ps. 19:1). The earth also belongs to God and we should not exploit or destroy the resources in it. The whole creation is also waiting for its redemption or renewal (Rom. 8: 18 -22). The whole of creation including animals, plants and humanity (The biotic and abiotic organisms and substances) are looking forward its ultimate liberation.

The greed and egocentrism (selfishness) which are caused by sin is the root cause of the ecological crisis. If we live only for ourselves, we fail to realize the ethics of care and to dig our own burial ground. A strong determination to control our egocentrism and anthropocentrism that only can help us to overcome our capitalistic, consumeristic and exploitative tendencies so that our resources can be preserved.

The industrialized nations only consist of 20 per cent of World's population is responsible for 75-80 per cent of annual Green House Gases emissions, which has to be regulated in order to avoid global warming and climate change. There is a distinction between "survival emission of the poor" and luxury emissions of the rich as it is stated, "Global warming brings into sharp focus the injustice of economic relationship between the North and the South. Excess consumption in the North, which is the root of the gobal warming problem, also deprives the south of sources necessary for development" (*Global Warming P.* 14). The eco-rights and eco-justice are important for keeping the integrity of creation. Water is an important resource, and without water no one can survive. Water should be used sparingly and responsibly. Take all measures to curb polluting water by human waste, chemical or unclear wastes. Rain harvest watershed programmes and keeping water in pools and ponds are to be promoted. The tapping of water especially ground water by the industrialists should be stopped. The ground water is also facing threat as this resource is also being dried up.

3

Towards a Terror-Free World

Terrorism is an extreme violent attitude developed by certain groups on religious, political or social grounds. They have an idea or aim of their own for which they are overzealous and intolerant and not relenting to use any means to achieve their goals. They are resorting to use guerilla warfare. Terrorism is an ideology, which achieves its goal by violent means. Terrorists may be a small group or a big movement. They achieve their aims by kidnapping persons, by use of explosives or by confrontation. They enter into arms fight with their opposing structures. Usually they rely on guerilla warfare. Terrorists bear the economic, political or religious banners.

The terrorism can be the outcome of the disgusted youths or adults who look for a fulfilment in life. They work for an order belonging to their vision and ideology. They also fight for a cause of their own. Terrorism is an attitude developed in an organized sense against certain authorities, which is found in the mind of human being. It is a fascism which challenges others in an intolerant manner. They enforce the law by the power of weapons. It is dictatorial. What is difficult to explain is, who has the authority to margin a group as terrorists. Terrorists fight for their cause sometimes without any sense. For example, they even kill many innocents without any reason.

Terrorism is like a war against the authorities whom

they do not like. When the World Trade Centre (USA) was demolished by a group it was called as a war of the terrorists - terrorist attacks. It took place in the month of September 2001, in which more than 6000 people died. America suspected the A1- Qaeda, a group-named as terrorists given lead by Osama Bin Laden. When certain Sikh group turned against Indian authorities, they are named as terrorists. Several Western countries and others like Pakistan, Israel and Palestinians involve in terrorist activities.

All the movements for justice is not terrorism. But terrorism usually is associated to violent attacks. It is more organized and they involve in more vehement attacks. Terrorists, sometimes, go against the common interests and they never yield for comporomise, except for their goals.

(1) The danger of terrorism is that they are indiscriminate and reckless where innocents may suffer.
(2) The violent attacks are not a means to achieve the goals. So dialogue should play a significant role to resolve problems.
(3) The terrorists can have any selfish goals which they enforce on others.
(4) It can bring disharmony and hatred in the society. It leads to destabilization.

The Latin world "terrere" means cause to tremble. Terrorism as the word indicates it causes fear or terror. Any extreme cruelty against another can be an act of terror. Historically it is found in war, ethnic conflicts, persecutions, invasions and vandalisms. Today, terrorists are widely understood as a fundamentalist group use violent means of attack against other religious communities, ideologies or countries. The terrorists involve in kidnapping, hijacking and brutal and reckless killing. The terrorist organization catch the youths by offering money, brainwash them and train them for guerilla warfare. The terrorists use all sophisticated weapons in their attack. Nature of their operation is indirect, subtle and rapid. There are state sponsored, and religious sponsored terrorisms. The Jehadi group like Lashkar - e- toiba and Taliban are based on a false understanding of the religion and especially the concept ' Jihad '. Sectarian religious extremist group are sometimes used by countries with a political motive.

The terrorists are adventurous and they are even willing to die for their cause as to appear in the form of human bomb or die in the encounter. One of the major terrorist attack India had witnessed was on 26th November, 2008 (26/11) in Bombay, mainly aimed at Taj Hotel, Oberoi Trident and Nariman House.

Terrorism is inhuman and it should be curbed. Martin Luther King III (son of Martin Luther King Jr) has stated that non-violence can be used effectively to tackle global terror. He argues, "The challenge today is to engage people also some characterise as terrorists, who certainly commit terrorist activities. How do we get them to understand that we must learn to live in a World without destroying persons or property. One of the ways to do that is through non-violence" [*The Hindu*, (Feb. 25, 2009), P. 1]. He continued to say, "we cannot start off condemning people for what they have done wrong. We have to reach out to them and understand their plight, try to get their trust. When we have done these things, we will be moving in the right direction" (*Ibid.*, P. 1) Martin Luther King III was very optimistic of non-violence by which terrorism can be tackled.

The teaching of the Bible is against terrorism. Shalom is visualizing a just world which takes care of the welfare of everyone. Kingdom of God is also peace with justice

(Rom 14:17) Jesus calls us to be peacemakers (Mt. 5). Apostle Paul also emphasizes the peace and reconciliation (1Cor. 5 : 18- 20). The structural problem such as justice, poverty, unemployment, and denial of rights and dignity are to be tackled in order to resolve the problem of terrorism. The religions should teach the essence of the religion than promoting a fundamentalist, extremist and terrorist attitude.

It is important to make realize everyone the evil of terrorism and its insensibility. An organized effort of religions, ideologies and other international and national bodies can help to make adequate responses to terrorism. Terrorism is menace to humanity, it has to be responded by everyone as they join in the organized endeavours. A discussion or peace-talk can be convened with the representatives of the terrorist groups in order to find amicable solution to the problems and to create harmony and understanding.

4

Ethnic Conflict - A Tyranny

The communities and races are to live together in harmony on this earth. Because of geographical or geopolitical factors different ethnic groups are formed and they claim distinct history, ancestory, language, sometimes religion and culture. Their backgrounds can be similar or even divergent. These racial or ethnic groups may even co-exist in a context. There is a tribal nature to these ethnic groups as they have their own claims and traditions. They also have a purity and superiority consciousnes.

The intolerant attitude, exclusive claims, economic disparity, struggle for political privileges and power, denial of rights, feeling of neglect, rejection and insecurity and other oppressive elements can lead to struggle for autonomy and ethnic conflict. The fascist tendencies are emerging in a greater way among human beings today. One of the major discussion is the ethnic identity and the life in unity. The human races conflict each other for their domination which create a disharmony in the whole world. The conflict between the Aryans and Dravidians can be identified as one of the earlier references for ethnic crises in India. The ethnic crises is the outcome of the intolerance and hatred among the races. This can lead to the genicode or the attempt of one race to annihilate the other race.

There is social, economic and political reasons behind the conflict between races. The Nazi attack against Jews in Germany is said to be (1) The claim of superiority of race by Jews, which the Germans never forbear (2) The economic accumulation by Jews was an eyesore before Germans. In order to achieve the fascist goal of German Nazis, they killed off 60 lakh Jews without any mercy. It was a terrorism against any human community. The ethnic crises in Srilanka was a longstanding one. The Singhalese and the Srilankan Tamils were in violent conflict. It is a racial conflict and, in turn, politically the war between the Liberation Tigers of Tamil Eelam (LTTE) and the Srilankan Government which was dominantly for autonomy and territorial integrity.

In South Africa there was ethnic crises as the blacks and whites entered into a conflict. The black argued for their meaningful political freedom which was gained through long years of struggle. The apartheid is a racial prejudice against blacks. In North America also it was practiced against blacks, the US minorities. It was by the powerful struggle under the leadership of Martin Luther King Jr and Malcolm X, the blacks gained their rights.

The racial conflict caused the division of Czechoslovakia and Yugoslavia. The Czechs and Slovaks were in violent conflict so also between croats and serbs. The superiority complex, the mobility or purity consciousness of certain races lead to the psychological war and later it enters into physical conflict and bloodshed. Tribalism is a major threat and ethnic conflict is so severe in African countries like Rwanda and Somalia where there is violence and genocide. There is mass-massacre in the name of race. In Rwanda, the Hutus and Tutsis involved in the ethnic war which created a terrific situation and thousands are killed within few days.

Bible affirms the harmonious extistence of all ethnic groups as all human beings are created in the image of God (Gen. 1:27; Gal. 3:28). The persons or communities belong to different races and background are to exist together (Ex. 20: 20-22). Jesus was concerned of the Samaritans (Jn. 4; LK. 10: 25ff) as he did accept their dignity and service though they are termed as outcastes by the Jews. The concept like justice, shalom, covenant and Kingdom of God stand for the pro-existence of ethnic groups. He recognized the identity, and dignity of the Cananites and the Romans (Mt. 15 :21ff; Lk. 7:1ff). The vision of the co-existence of the different ethnic groups in the community of God is given to Peter (Acts. 10: 9ff). Bible is not for ethnic conflict but for the peaceful living of ethnic groups. The following principles are important for the co-existence of ethnic groups.

(1) Conscientize the people to live with the principle of mutuality. It is important to have meaningful participation to all races.

(2) Discourage the tendency to dominate other racial groups. Live in amity by accepting the racial diversity.

(3) Accept the fact that every human being is related and the humanity is one. So hating and annihilating each other is a violence done against one's own family members and against God, who created everyone in his image.

5

Conflicts, Wars and Weapons

The World had witnessed two great World Wars and their atrocities. The worst of their consequence was the bombing of Hiroshima and Nagasaki (both in Japan) in the World War II. The people of the country of Japan are still suffering from that terrible act of United States and its allies. The former President of America, George Bush had confessed that it was an act of terror. He apologized for it. Anyone can apologize after any insensible, irresponsible and immature and deliberate inhuman act, but what about redeeming the people from consequences ?. The bombs that were dropped at Hiroshima and Nagasaki were Atom Bombs. Now, there are more terrible Nuclear Weapons. So it is very important to dwell upon this issue of arm-race.

Science and Technology are originally meant for the total progress of humanity. They are to be used to improve the quality of life of mankind. Unfortunately, these are used to annihilate the weak. When two countries are equally good in their military power they never go for testing their strength because of the sheer fear. If some countries are found to be weak, the powerful ones try to attack them. This is what exactly America and its allied countries are doing today. If we recall the Gulf War (Iraq vs. US and allies), we will realize that what US and its gang done was totally reprehensible. They had bombarded the cities and have caused severe harm to the common people. The innocent people including women and babies were killed. Women and children are usually the victims of war, communal riots or any disturbances of this sort. The wars have become a fight between common people and soldiers rather than between soldiers. Indiscriminate kind of wars have made the life of humanity miserable.

Atomic power has been used for many years in warfare. The nuclear weapons kill thousands in seconds through the bomb blast and other explosive elements. Japan is suffering the consequences of the American bombing in the World War II. The radioactive elements are affecting badly even the newly born children, which bring genetic disorders. All nuclear powers are conducting the nuclear tests which even pollute the atmosphere and wipe out thousands of living organisms which upholds the ecological equilibrium. The explosion and the radioactve elements do harm the life of the plants, animals and human beings.

The biological weapons are said to be more dangerous than chemical and unclear weapons. The chemicals or toxic elements are used in the chemical warfare which kills when one inhales the toxic chemical substance. It is the severe threat to the existence of humanity. The Bio- weapons are a threat to humanity. It is observed that biological weapons are easy to make and easily available. The most potential bio-weapons category includes the anthrax, plague, Tularaemia, small pox, and Ebola- influenza hybrid. These bacterias can inflict heavy tolls. The terrorists are using these weapons against their enemies in order to offend them in the Afgan-US War (2001- 2002), the anthrax was used by Afgan-centred terrorists. The innocents will be also affected by the use of bio-weapons.

War is a crime against humanity. It should not be promoted. Those who involve in war and other innocents will be adversely affected by war. It is also a waste of money. It creates ecological disaster and the whole creation will be affected by war. Pollution of air, loss of life and famine and pestilence are the consequences of war, so war is inhuman.

The amount of money used for Nuclear and other kinds of sophisticated weapons are unpardonably high. Instead of bringing happiness, peace and harmony, money is used to buy weapons to cause misery, famine, disease and death. More people and countries are fabricating strategies to exploit and to cause harm to others rather than bringing up life and welfare for the humanity. While there are crucial problems like poverty, malnutrition, epidemics, unemployment and other injustices, it is quite unfortunate that our priorities are set on arm-struggle and cold war. Wars have made the life of human beings miserable, and people are between the life and death struggle. The words of the tireless apostle of lepers Raoul Follereau are very significant to be recalled. He said: "Just give me the money for a single atomic bomber, and I will care the fifteen million lepers on this planet." (Quoted in *Beyond Love* by Dominique Lapierre, P. 36).

The war between the rival factions in and the different countries are the most horrible ones today. Wars are making this world a hell. The common people are moving to different places for security reasons. They have to run for life. Wars begin in human hearts, told Leo Tolstoy. This is a true statement 'Wars are fought to conquer and to take revenge.' So War is antithetical to peace. It is ridiculous to combine a slogan like. 'War is for peace'. Violence, indeed, will breed violence, and it will bring more misery to humanity. 'War is for destruction'. War will not resolve any problems, since it promotes hatred and rivalry. Charles Curran, the America moral Theologian, recognized the great need and importance of peace for good of all human beings. For him, the use of nuclear weapons is totally wrong, and the just war theory is a deception. He suggests that violence or force can be used only against the bearers of force. For him the whole Christian message is to achieve peace and justice in the society (*Ongoing Revision in Moral Theology* PP. 165-172). The Indian religious traditions also have given utmost importance to the principles ' do not harm ' and '*Shanti*' (peace). Buddhism and Jainism have been the greatest challenge in this regard. The tenets of these religions uphold the principle of non-violence. Hinduism also emphasizes the principle of *Ahimsa* (non-violence).

The whole Christian message is one of love, peace and compassion (Mathew 5:38-44). Buddha also hails compassion. He said, "Only virtue gives a good Karma and the greatest of all virtue is compassion". Unless we are moved by the love and compassion, the world would be doomed by the terrors of war, strife and riots. The Brotherhood of mankind has to be accepted by all in order to overcome the enemity. 'Shalom'(peace) should be the catchword and not war. While war is destructive '*Shanti*' is creative. Upholding ' *Shanti*' is the need of the time. Jesus called us to become peace-makers.

6

Women and their issues

The gender issue is one of the serious issues in the world. Though there are efforts made for the empowerment of women, the gender based prejudices and discriminations are found everywhere. The structure of patriarchy denies the identity, dignity, status and rights of women

Patriarchy

Patriarchy or male-chauvinism is a structural evil that brings an unequal ralationship in the name of gender. The inferiority of women was advocated by Greek, Roman, Semitic and Asian cultures. In Indian society, the birth of a boy is received joyfully, but birth of a girl makes everyone sad. Women are like out castes, dalits and marginalized. Menstruation of women is understood as pollution. There is victimization as there are domestic violence, sexual offense from the society and discrimination in the field of economics and politics. They have no power as the income generating resources are held by men. The culture also dehumanizes them as the customs and manners, are male - dominated. The customs, proverbs and attitudes are meant for respecting men and not women.

The women are less regarded compared to men in the Indian society. The condition of poor women, dalit women and tribal women are still worse. Their labour power is exploited and sexually offended as the patriarchal society recognize women only as objects. They are only considered as sex-tools. It is like women are to be used, abused and divorced according to the will of men.

In the Greek, Roman and Semitic cultures, the role and status of women are considered inferior to men. They are only puppets in the hands of men. Their rights are denied and they are devalued. In all societies, including the Western society, the girls and women are molested, raped, physically tortured, and treated inhumanly. There is discrimination in power-sharing, participation in decision-making and in opportunities. These are also the expressions of patriarchy.

Violence against women

In all areas of life the women are most victimized as violence is used by society against them. They are quite alienated everywhere and there is systemic violence against them. Ignoring, neglecting, abusing, objectifying and torturing them are all part and parcel of violence done against them. The patriarchal society is not concerned of protecting and safeguarding women. The attitudes such as 'commodity' and 'object' over women is a disastrous concept which consider women as a sex tool to abuse. The female is reduced to an object of lust to male members.

The women and girls are harassed sexually and physically assaulted from the domestic situation and by the society. The dowry deaths, gang rape, wife battering, desertion by husbands, ill-treatment in the old age are some of the violence they suffer. In the work place also the women are harassed, sexually assaulted, physically and mentally tortured. There are even cases of forcing the dalit women to walk naked in public. The dalit women were also sexually exploited and killed by the dominant class. Women and children are kidnapped which is a violent infringement on personal space and freedom. The girls are not even safe in the womb of the mother as there is female foeticide.

The Indian Constitution and Indian Penal Code is clear on the security or protection of girls and women. The protection of women from Domestic Violence Act, 2005 is to safeguard the women who are subjected to domestic violence. But the negligence of the protection officer or service provider and the police do prevent to furnish justice to the victimized women

The Constitution of India (Articles 14, 15, 39a, b, c; 51) guarantees the protection of law. It also condemned discrimination in the name of gender. Their dignity and rights are affirmed. The Factories Act, 1948 protects the women at the work place. The rape, kidnapping and offences against women for dowry are prohibited by the law. But it is so happened that the women are not getting justice from the society and legal system. The patriarchal dominance that appears in the form of policemen, Magistrates and members of the society are to justify the crime against girls and women. Violence against women is a crime which is to be curbed. Those who are in power sometimes ignore the seriousness of the evil deeds against women.

Dowry System

Dowry related harassments, torture and deaths are common in the Indian society. It questions the identity, dignity and rights of women as they are objectified and exploited for the sake of monetary benefits. The humanity of women are not recognized in the bargaining. Women are understood as secondary citizens by some cultures. The Greeks have considered them as property. Their personhood was not recognized by them. In the Jewish context also the women are categorized as an inferior being.

The Jewish Rabbis thank God for not being born as a woman. In the Asian situation also the women have been considered as inferior to men. The male domination is a commonscene in almost all societies. But this inferior status of women is changing slowly. Dowry system is an evil practice because it involves the bargaining and the rejection of the girls from the poor background. The dowry system badly affects the people from the lower strata of the society, and it does much harm to them rich. Dowry system itself is probably, a creation of the male dominated society. The dowry system brings about a competition among the rich, and in this competition the poor cannot reach anywhere.

The dowry system terribly divides the mankind. It creates a disharmony and hatred among the human beings, It is true that the girls should get their due share, but do all girls have share ? All girls may not have a big share. The girls from the poor economic background may not have any share at all. Most of the girls are belonging to this group in India. In this condition, it is important to think about the dowry system. The wives are beaten and even killed by the husbands or their relatives. So many brides are burnt or tortured since the bridegrooms are not satisfied of the amount of the dowry. Many women are tortured mentally by the husbands and relatives. Women are also sent back to their home because of dowry claims. Marriage has degenerated as a greed for money.

Because of the dowry system the society as a whole is keeping a negative attitude towards girl children. When a baby girl is born everybody will have a gloomy face. There would not be any joy at the birth of baby girl unlike the birth of baby boy. It is solely because of the dowry system, the girl children are killed by the community of Thevars at Uslampatti near Madurai in Tamilnadu. We may condemn these practices, but fail to ask why ? We ignore the social realities by making some lame excuses. In 1986 around 1, 319 dowry- deaths were recorded, says Dr. Somen Das (*Christian Ethics and Indian Ethos* p. 27). The dowry-deaths are on the increase and it is not declining. It should be kept in mind that so many instances of wife burning and dowry deaths are not registered. These serious crimes are to be curbed. This is an inhuman act. This is demonic.

Though the Indian Constitution furnishes equal status to women and men, the discriminations are going on without any shame. Donna exposes the evils of dowry system. She says, "young women within short spans of three months to five years of a married life are burnt to death, drowned, strangled and driven to suicide unable to fight the privatized violence within the walls of the house" (*Towards a Theology of Humanhood: Women's Perspective,* P. 10). The girls who are yet to be married are a liability to the family. The violence against women because of dowry issue is a common evil in the system. Periyar E. V. Ramaswamy has opined that the 'women should be given equal right along with men for the family property". (*Periyar:Father of the Tamil Race,* p. 31). He was also against the dowry system and the discrimination towards women.

Dowry system brings a social disorganization in the society. It is also a symbol of degeneration. A new value system has to be developed in order to challenge the demonic structure of the society. Eradication of the unjust practices is a human responsibility. Dowry system makes the life of the poor impossible. The utter selfishness of the dominant class always prefer to have a *status quo* in the society, since they are so benefitted by the present system. But it is just to criticize the evils of the structure to bring out a transformation in the society.

The problems of dowry system are quite significant to be specified.

(1) It affirms the inferior status of women.

(2) Dowry system does affect badly the life of the poor people

(3) It enable the society to develop a negative attitude to girl children

(4) Dowry system brings disharmony in husband - wife relationship, and even in the life of the whole family

(5) This oppressive system can lead to torture over women

(6) The dowry system gives psychological torture to girls and the parents.

Dowry come into existence as gift (Hebrew 'Mohar') but it is reduced to be an exploitative means as a result of male domination. Mohar is bridal money or bridal price (Gen. 34: 12, Ex22, 16-17). It is given as wedding gift (Num 18:11, prov. 18:16; 19:6; 24:14). The sum of money paid by the bridegroom to the bride's family at the time of betrothal, from this point onwards the marriage is legally in force. In Indian context, it is expected from girls only. Since the Biblical vision is against any indignity and exploitation, it is important to curb this social evil. It does a lot of harm to womenhood in the form of oppression, so dowry system should be challenged.

Dowry system is a dehumanizing and oppressive element which objectifies women and oppress them. As it challenges the womenhood and oppress them it has to be opposed. God opposes the dehumanizing elements and sides the victimized (Jere 5:26-28;Ezk 18:12-17;1Jn 3:10). Bargaining in the marriage for money and avoiding women as they are not financially sound (Sense that they are not having the expected amount of money) are injustices. So it is important to protest this social evil. The persons, Churches, Government and other voluntary organizations should challenge the dowry system. The poor women are severely victimized so it is significant to support them and to work for their emancipation. The money factor in marriage should go and the'care and love factor'should come in order to tackle the dowry system.

The women confront several problems from the patriarchal society. Their identity, dignity and rights are not recognized and they are also considered as objects. They also suffer different kinds of violence which dehumanize them. So it is important to respond to these issues and to affirm justice.

7

Gender Pluralism or Diversity and the Crises

There is a gender pluralism or divide and a diverse gender issues found. There is genetic divide so also socio-economic divide. Human being can be divided into man, women and transgender (Trans men and Trans women). There are elite women or women belong the dominant class and women who belong to the subaltern groups such as dalit, tribal and black women. However, in patriarchal society, women are vulnerable victimized and powerless. Each category of women have their own crises and struggles. They are seeking their identity, dignity and rights .

I. The Plight of Women

The patriarchal structure has contributed so much to the plight for women. The male-dominated society does not recognize identity, dignity and rights of women. Male chauvinism does also go to the extreme by which it silences and victimizes women. Their role and status are limited by the society, so there is no meaningful participation of women in decision-making. They are forced to stay as passive members in the domestic situation and in the community. Everywhere we could see a gender 'apartheid' or discrimination and prejudice against women. They are objectified and merely understood as a sex-tool .

The girls and women are kidnapped for sexual abuse, and they are raped . The sexual assault is a common cruelty against women. There are also cases of gang rape which is a torture against women. The devadasi system and sati are not yet wiped out from the Indian scene. In the context of communal riots also the women are sexually assaulted. They are insecure in the domestic situation and also in the society. Socially, economically and politically the women are powerless.

According to Felix Wilfred, there are certain issues of primary importance in relation to Asian women. They are the practice of sati, dowry and the legitimisation of women's subjugation by religious and cultural traditions *(Asian Dreams and Christian hope at the Dawn of the millennium,* New Delhi: ISPCK, 2000. P. 145). He continues to narrate the plight of women by telling that, "In South Asia, the burden of traditional dowry system has been further aggravated with modern capitalist consideration of money and profit. What is happening is a commerce of women and when she proves unable to increase one's capital, there is least hesitation to physically assault her and even consign her to consuming flames"(*Ibid.* , P. 147).

The girl child is a liability, so they are got rid of by infanticide or by sex-selection test like amniocentesis. There is a decline in male/female ratio. Amartya Sen speaks of one hundred million "missing women" in Asia and Africa (*Ibid.* , P. 147). The women are oppressed in different ways. The patriarchal structure is subjugating them to make them an object of sex and exploit their potential for low wages. Even the girl chldren are forced to do hard work. They are also the victims of molestation and abuse of sex.

According to Felix Wilfred, "A primary form of violence against dalits is to rape and humiliate their women. Innumerable cases of violence against dalits have resulted in raping Dalit women, and in many cases parading them naked"(*Dalit Empowerment*, Delhi; ISPCK, 2007, 97). The Dalit women are continuously raped, killed and harassed by patriarchal structures, especially the upper castes. Their identity, dignity and rights are denied. They are the victims of gender-injustice.

In the words of Asangla Lemtur, "Generally, tribal ethos and customs are also patriarchal that dehumanize the identity of women" "An ethical Analysis of the Tribal ethnic identity - crises in India; A Feminist Critique" *Religion and Society* vol. 50, No. 3 (September 2005, P. 79). There are traces of patriarchy such as low status, subordination and oppression are found in tribal contexts. Compared to the hill tribes of North East India, the identity, dignity and rights of other tribes are only less recognized. They are the victims of sexual assault, evacuation from habitat in the name of development. They are socially, economically and politically powerless (C. S. Chandrika, *Arthavamulla Sthreekal*, Malayalam Book, English translation can be *the potent women)* Mavelikara : Fabian Books, 2008. PP. 19, 57, 6366).

The tribals are exploited by the private individuals or groups. The money-lenders, forest contractors and Government officials have entered the tribal world to claim their shares of tribal resources (N. K . Vaid, *Who Cares for Tribal Development*, New Delhi, Mittal Publications, 2004. p. 3). N. K. Vaid states again "Forest policy was reoriented dissociating tribal from land which is not only their source of livelihood but also a very vital aspect of their Cultural and Psychological make-up. Gradually they were uprooted – Socially, Culturally, Economically, Politically, Ritually, Psychologically, and Physically. Tribal has a hazy future-nay, dark future-nay no future at all" (*Ibid.* , P. 3). It is observed that more than three quarters of Scheduled Tribes women are illiterate and the male Scheduled Tribes literacy rate is 29.60 per cent (*Ibid.* , P. 9).

The forceful trafficking of girls and women for sex work is also very common in the Indian context. Tourism is also reduced to be sex-tourism, so the sex became an indispensable factor, where women are objectified for the interests of the patriarchy. The structural problem such as poverty or financial crisis also forces women to sell their bodies for livelihood.

The condition of women are not promising in the cultural and religious contexts as the language, customs and structures are highly patriarchal. The attitudes, saying (e.g. proverbs) and practices are gender-biased. In the ecclesiastical context also women role is limited. The opportunities are denied to women, especially in leadership positions.

II. Gender Divide: Issues and the Debate

The women are also plural in nature and status as they are representing different socio-economic realities. The transgender issues and the sex work are also the major debates today. The identity, dignity and right of women are in question and it is explored from selected issues for furnishing possible suggestions as solutions. Political equality, economic equality, gender justice and transgender issues are the major concerns in this research.

(a) *Political inequality and empowerment.*

One of the feminist concerns is the political rights of women. They look forward their meaningful participation and involvement in politics. Their role in the decision making is a great concern. In Indian context the 33 per cent Reservation or quota for women in Parliament, Legislative Assemblies and in local administration (e.g. Panchayats) are demanded but it is not yet worked out in

Parliament and Legislative Assemblies. It is observed by Mythiliy Sivaraman that women occupy far less than 10 per cent of positions in High Court and Supreme Court and 3 per cent in Govt. administratin and management positions ("changing women equations - a gender perspective" *Jecvadhara* vol. XXXVIII, No. 223, (January 2008), P. 5).

It is clear that power sharing is unequal or there is a gender divide in India. The women are not having equal power with men. The feminist movements in United States of America also emphasize the next most important battle as equality in power . Though there are improvement in women's role and participation in some sectors like journalism, it is stated by Ms. Jodi Enda, the programme planner for the knight centre for specialized Journalism in Washington DC, that "people who run things in the United States, be it in the Government or Corporations, are men" (Cited in "US feminist movement undergoing generational shift:Jodi Enda" by Sruthi Krishnan. *The Hindu,* October 22, 2008. P. 16) Jodi Enda continued to say "we have won the battle for equality in numbers. The next is equality in power" (*Ibid.* , P . 16).

The politics today is an androcentric politics where women participation is very minimal. The female voices are neglected and silenced by the forces of male - chauvinism, especially in the decision-making bodies, so they have no involvement in the policy-making.

The Dalit women are politically conscious of their rights, so they are organizing and moblizing themselves against the gender-injustices. They are mostly agricultural labourers in unorganized sector. They are not adequately represented in women or dalit movements. In 1987 Ruth Memorama organized the women in Bangalore and it gives rise to 'National Federation of Dalit Women' which stood for the rights of Dalit Women (M. Hilaria Soundari. *Dalit Women : Dimension of Empowerment,* Dindigul : Vaigarai

Pathippagam, 2006. PP. 40-41). The Tamilnadu dalit women movement also raised questions related to violence against dalit women, impact of globalization and the rights (*Ibid.*, P. 41). The Dalit women are also conscious of their constitutional, legal, political rights and demanding from the Government to appropriate the same.

According to Nirmal Minz, "In my perecption, perspective and understanding tribal people in general are facing situation in which their very existence, identity and survival are questioned. Some really concerned persons feel, if the situation and conditions prevailing among the tribals continue for few decades more as they are now, many tribal communities will disappear from the list of the Government of India" "Tribal issues in India today" *Religion and Society* Vol. 50. No. 3 (September 2005), P. 3). As the tribals are powerless the political structure is also suppressing them and denying their rights.

As Asangla Lemtur observes, "An analysis of the tribal situation also point to the fact that, the tribal women face mutiple dehumanizations through sexism, racism and classism. She is suppressed not only as a tribal, more so by the patriarchal male-dominated culture" "An Ethical Analysis of the Tribal Ethnic Identity Crisis in India : A feminist Critique" *Religion and Society* (September 2005), PP. 64-65. The general observation is that the 'tribal ethos and customs are also patriarchal that de-humanize the identity of women' (*Ibid.*, p. 79). The tribal women are for politcal empowerment as they sing the song (the tribal women of Maharashtra). 'Let us enter politics, continue our struggle and take leadership' (Vibhuti Patel, "Getting a Foothold in Politics. . . . women in politcal decision - making process" *Social Action* Vol. 55, No. 1 (January - March 2005, P. 37). "This song", according to Vibhuti Patel, "represented the new understanding of 'politics'. Politics as not only electoral politics or membership in political parties, but as a collective action of women against oppressive patriarchal power with a long term goal of social transformation that ensured women liberation from exploitation, degradation, injustice, subjugation and superstition, casteism and communalism" (*Ibid.* , p. 37). Vibhuti Patel is arguing for participation of tribal and other marginated women in decision-making bodies.

(b) Economic Inequality

The gender-divide is also found in the area of economics. The access to economic resources is quite minimal for women compared to men. There is discrimination in employment opportunities and also in wages. It is noticed that though there is an economic growth in Asia, it is overshadowed by uneven progress and disparities glaringly visible between countries in the region, within countries, and between their men/ boys and women/girls states Dr. Noeleen Heyzer ("Gender inequalities must be tackled if MDGs are to be achieved" *The Hindu*, September 24, 2008. P. 11. MDGs is Millennium development goals. It is a UN plan for the development of Asia-pacific region).

In certain sector the opportunites for women are curbed. It is noted in engineering sector that the women are not very much recruited. According to Mythiliy Sivaraman, "The study also found that it is harder for women engineers to find jobs, and unemployment was higher among them than among men. Some companies coming for campus recruitment openly stated that they will not take female engineers and most interviewers were not even aware of the legal implication of questioning women candidates differently" (Op. Cit. P. 15).

Though the Government of India enacted a law to pay equal payment for equal work, in the non-Governmental and unorganized sector the women are not given equal payment for equal work compared to men. There is exploitation and oppression of women in the economic sphere. This provides the picture that women's status and rights are not regarded by the patriarchal society. The objectification and dehumanization of women are found in economic realm where women rights are denied. The patriarchal society is not ready to accept the dignity and the potentiality of women. It is also to be noted that in the non-organized and non-Governmental sector, the women who work are mostly from dalit and tribal background, so they are victimized much.

According to Crystal David John, faculty of the Department of Economics, Stella Maria College, Chennai, 'Economics has been profoundly prejudiced by the high value masculine attitude. This is evident from the very assumptions in the subject. This then is bolstered together by male centred methodology" ["Challenge to Adrocentric Economics" *Jeevadhara*, Vol. XXXVIII, No. 223 (January 2008), P. 49]. It is noted that economic theories are lopsided in its analysis of real life situation. She continued to state, "This occurs because such theories have turned their back on women. Subject that are vital for women, such as their position in the labour market in relation to men, the economic value of household work, and the numerous caring and nurturing jobs they perform have never been part of the scope of Economic Theory"(*Ibid.*, P. 49). So it is important to restructure and re-orient economics from the feminist point of view which would uphold the role, status and impact of women in the sector of Economics.

According to M. Hilaria Soundari, "among women visibly the pyramid structure of Indian society portrays that dalit women are in the lowest socio-economic strata of society"(*Dalit Women : Dimension of Empowerment*, Dindigul : Vaigarai Pathippagam, 2006. p. 19). The dalit women are understood as the downtrodden among the downtrodden . She continued to state, "Struggles of dalit women are formidable in a male-dominated deprived society . They are looked down on as dependent, weak and powerless" (*Ibid.* , p. 19). It is observed by Soundari that Amartya Sen has indicated gender inequality as not one homogenous phenomenon, but a collection of desperate and interlinked problems and different kinds of gender equality are displayed in morality, natality, basic facility, special opportunity professions, ownership and even household matters. Gender disparity includes the discrimination of Dalit women as well (*Ibid.* , P. 20).

There is clear indication from the study of tribal women that there is a degradation in their status which is measured in terms of household burden, starvation, health hazards, harassment by male members and low wages. Even for some hard work, they are only getting rupees twenty or less than twenty rupees per day (This is the observation made by Walter Fernandes, Geeta Menon and Gail Omvedt as they study on Tribals of Orissa and Kalahandi District [cited in "deforestation and tribal under development : fact from Kalahandi district of Orissa" by Kunj Bihari Nayak *Social Action* vol. 54, No. 1 (January - March 2004), P. 83]. It is also reported that the tribal women get only Rs. 15/- per day for road construction and Rs. 10/- per day for agricultural works (*Ibid .* , p. 83). It is clear that the tribal women are victims of economic inequality. They are deceived by Government agencies, the middlemen and landlords.

There are cases reported that when there is draughts and scarcity of resources, the male members migrate to cities like Delhi, Mumbai and Nagpur in search of work and livelihood, the poor tribal women and children at home face threats of hunger, manlnutrition and epidemics and some of them even die (*Ibid.* , P. 85). This shows the gravity of problem the tribal women face as there is gross economic inequality.

The economic rights of women are to be upheld and they are to be empowered . The subaltern women are the worst victims of economic disparities. The dalit, tribal and black women are extremely marginated and powerless politically, socially, economically and gender-wise. They are not benefitted by the economic growth. The privileges and rights are usually gained by the elite men and women. Even among the gender-prejudice, the victimization of the poor and marginalized or non-elite women is a serious concern. Unless very serious efforts are taken to educate, conscientize and organize them, the empowerment is not possible. They should be given opportunities to exercise their potential and to have access to the income-generating resources.

The Global Gender Gap Report 2008 published by World Economics forum points out that the Nordic countries (Norway, Finland and Sweden), topped this year's score as measuring equality between men and women in 130 countries. It is observed that no country closed fully 'the gap between men and women when it comes to economic paticipation and opportunity, educational attainment, political enpowerment and health and survival' [*The Hindu* (November 16, 2008), P. 18]. The conidition of India is quite worse in relation to closing the economic gap between men and women as India is ranked only 113 out of total of 130 countries. It is suggested that representation of women in senior leadership position, economic and political participation, educational attainment and income equality are essential to narrow down the economic gap between men and women (*Ibid.*, P. 18).

(c) Women-sexual and marital issues

In marital relations also the gender discriminations are found. The gender divide is found as there is bias in relation to women's dignity and status . The equal status of women with men is not reorganized and this is found in the forms of wife battering, dowry deaths, desertion and irresponsible divorces.

The women are also considered as a sex object. They are sexually abused and assaulted . Even the girl children are widely used for sexual gratification. Women are raped, even gang raped and the society and Government machinery is silent on these issues as it happened in the case of some women who are sexually assaulted in the context of persecution of Christians in Orissa. Recently the High Court of Kerala came strongly against indiscreet divorces. It urged, especially the Muslim Community to set up regional and central bodies to control and supervise Muslim marriage and divorce. The system is to avoid the indiscreet marriages and divorce. The Court observed that according to Quran the polygamy was allowed only in the situation where there are lot of widows, orphans and captives of war who were unable to maintain a dignified life (*The Hindu*, October 23, 2008, P. 1). These observations were made in the wake of men enjoy the unrestricted freedom to marry the women of their choice and pronounce *talaq* according to their whims and fancies (*Ibid.*, P. 1). There is gender-divide in the issue of marriage as men take advantage over women to divorce them without adequate reasons. The discriminatory attitude towards women in all areas of life, including sex and marital relations are to be curbed as they are anti-religious and inhuman. The Law Commision also enforced the registration of divorce as there are out-of-court divorce which provides abundant room for misuse of law and causes great hardships to women (*The Hindu*, October 20, 2008, P. 13).

It is reported, "In India's Southern states, thousands of girls are forced into prostitution before reaching the age of puberty. Devadasis literally meaning "female servant of God", usually belong to the dalit community. Once dedicated, the girl is unable to marry, forced to become a prostitute for upper-caste community member, and eventually auctioned off to an urban brothel"(Smitha Narula, *Broken People*, Bangalore : Books for change, 2001. p. 9). Human Rights watch (A human right organization) has observed that the dailt girls have been forced to have sex with the village landlord and dailt women are raped as a form of retaliation. It is noted that the "women of scheduled castes and scheduled tribes are raped as part of an effort by upper-caste leaders to suppress movement to demand payment of minimum wages, to settle sharecropping disputes, or reclaim lost land . They are raped by the upper caste, by landlords, and by the police in pursuit of their male relatives" (*Ibid.* , P. 31).

The sexual harassment in the work place is also a common factor. It is noted by Siddhartha Sarkar that 'the verbal sexual haassment by male employers is generally very common' ["Gender, work and informity : A Comparative study of female domestic and *Bidi* workers "*Social Action*, vol. 55, No. 4 (October- December 2005) P. 375.]. This is a common factor that the women employees are harassed and sexually abused by employers and fellow employees. The women are also facing domestic violence in developed and developing countries, observed by the United Nations General Assembly 1991 ["Domestic violence against women : Emerging Concerns in Rural Haryana" by Neerja Ahlawat, *Social Action* (October-December 2005), P. 387]. Neerja Ahlawat stated, "Domestic Violence aganist women is widely prevalent in both developed and developing societies. The abuse of women by men is among the most common and dangerous forms of gender based violence"(*Ibid.* , P. 387). She continues to indicate that domestic violence involves physical, sexual, psychological and economic brutality. Physical abuse includes slapping and beating and the sexual abuse include the unwanted touching, showing undesirable pictures forcefully, forcing to engage in undesirable sex and forced sexual acts. There are several other issues like wife-battering, sexual abuse of female children, dowry related violence, rape, including marital rape (*Ibid* . , P . 391).

(d) Women and sex work

Sex is very much commercialized. The media is also celebrating it in the magazines, cinema and advertisement. The art, architecture and literature (Stories and Novels) are also making use of the female sex as an object of pleasure. The female body is used for commercial purpose. For the advertisement of the products, the companies are opting to use female bodies with a sex appeal.

The tourism is also reduced to be sex tourism as the main attraction for tourism is the sex. Women are used as an object to attract tourism. There are situations where the women are forced to involve in sex work as there is economic crises. The poverty, unemployment and desertions can be the conditions by which one may become a sex- worker. The sex workers are now organized and they demand dignity and rights. They are exploited and assaulted by brothel-keepers, the clients and policemen. They also live in unhealthy living conditions.

Nalini Jameela was born in Trichur became the member of Kerala sex workers forum (Anasuya) from the year 2000 onwards . She was narrating her story (experience) in the book 'Oru Laingika Thozhlilaliyule Atmakatha' in Malayalam ("Autobiography of a sex-worker"), which was compiled by I. Gopinath, and published by D. C. Books, Kottayam, in the year 2005. In this book Punathil Kunjabdulla, the writer observes that even as religions and state laws condemn the sex work as an immoral thing, the commercial sex work continues.

Nalini Jameela states that she is sexually free as there are domestic violence and sexual assaults in marital life. She argues that the sex work is not inferior compared to the work of a teacher or a scientist (*Ibid.,* PP. 15 - 16). She was a victim of several marriages and divorces and she was considered by the ' husbands 'as a sex object . She was assaulted by *gundas* and even policemen (*Ibid.* , PP. 27 ff).

'Jwalamukhi'was an organization for the sex workers rights based in Trichur (Kerala State). They organized classes to conscientize them, especially on the sexually trasmitted diseases like HIV /AIDS. The sex workers also gather to share their experiences (*Ibid.* , P. 70). According to Jean D' Cunha there are social reasons for female sex work. They include ill-tretment of relatives, poverty, destitution, deception, kidnapping, heredity and environmental influence (*The Legalization of Prostitution*, Bangalore: CISRS, 1991. P. 4). Sex work can be defined as a professional sexual service for payment, states Kathleen Barey (*Ibid.* , P. 17).

A certain section of sex workers argue that it is a dignified job like any other job. It is understood as a great service to humanity by them. It is a decent job states Normajin Almador as it is better than any other job in a corrupt department (she was referring to police department, from where she resigned to choose to become a sex worker). But C. S. Chandrika was asking, how a sex worker is free as she is assaulted by gundas and police. In her observation she is also reduced to be an object of men's violence and her sex is controlled by men (*Arthavamulla Sthreekal,* a Malayalam book entitled 'the potent Women' by C. S Chandrika, Mavelikara : Fabian Books, 2008, P. 93). The globalization also forces women to be part of commerce and market to sell their bodies for pleasure of men to gain money. There are trafficking of women and even girl children for the sake of sex work. It is important to redeem them from their plight. It is victimization of a gender, the powerless and poor women who should be conscientized, restored and rehabilitated to normal life. This marginalized groups are the victims of evil and unjust structures, so they are to be liberated from their crisis.

(e) *The Crisis of Transgenders*

It is observed that there are one million transgenders or

the 'third sex ' in India. There is first sex (male), second sex (female) and third sex (transgenders). Burma or Myanmar has the largest transgender community and then comes India. Transgenders are named as Eunuchs, Aravanis, Androgyne, Ladyboys, Hijada, Omnigenders, Gender Queer, third gender and third sex.

According to Charles Edwin the cause of being a transgender is described as follows: "This condition is due to inaccurate division of chromosomes in the genes in the foetus during the ninth week of the pregnancy. The child then develops the qualities of both male and female. Though the child is born with the male genital organ, the qualities of the female child slowly become obvious at the age of six to eight years . "The church's Response to Third sex" *NCCI Review* (March 2005, P. 36). The children find psycho-social problems as they are neglected and marginalized during social interactions and family gathering and is treated as an unwanted child (*Ibid.* , P. 36) This results is running away from home to find their identity and aspiration in their own group. For this, they may also get the help of seniors.

The transgenders are divided into two groups : (1) Transmen - Men trapped in women body, (2) Transwomen -Women trapped in men body. The biological issue of transgenders lead to psycho-social problems. How the transgenders are born ? Elaine Storkey observed that the disorder 'S alpha-reductese deficiency' (an enzyme deficiency) results in genetic males being born with genitalia of female appearance. There is an ambiguity about sexuality until the puberty. When masculinity occurs they are not able to cope with the disorder as they are raised as girls. The similar problem is also found among genetically female children who are born with masculinised genitalia. They also do face the confusion of identity. It is observed that there is an increased incidence of lesbianism in women with this disorder (*Men and Women created or constructed.* Secunderabad: OM Authentic Books, 2001. P. 23).

The experience of a 'Hijada, 'a transgender when visited Kerala is important to note here. She / he is Lakshmi Narayanan Tripati who is member of UN Civil Society's Mission and active in the organization called 'Asian - pacific sex workers net work' which is based in Malaysia. She / he has a dance group includes male and female Hijadas and Lakshmi also run a voluntary organization calls ' Asthitva' in Thane (near Bombay, India) . She said that everybody was staring at her as a wonderful object as she visited Kerala . Lakshmi also states that the Government has a negligent attitude towords them. Lakshmi also points that even Shabna Mausic, the *Hijada* member of the Parliament also didnot do anything good for them (Malayala Manorama (Daily Newspaper) Sept. 24, 2008. P. 5).

Similar story is also told by Subair, who is a transgender. Appeared as a woman as Subair has the traits of a woman. She states that the brothers did not accept Subair's female traits, and did not even like to talk or discuss things with her even as they take crucial decisions. Subair was identified with girls and not with boys. Though Subair was talented in singing and dancing everyone was mocking at Subair which leads to dropping school education. Subair had even asked questions like why only I am created like this ? Even as her identity was not accepted by family and society, she chose to become a sex worker. As a sex worker Subair was assaulted by physically policemen and sexually by men (Clients). Subair narrates that they find identity in their groups and organization which are found in Kannur, Calicut, Trivandram and Ernakulam (Kerala). They are also well organized in Kolkata and Bombay. Subair states that they (transgenders-third sex) are neglected and oppressed groups who are slowly alienated (Pachakkuthira (Malayalam Journal) December 2005-PP. 53- 57). Subair, the transman was trying to open our eyes to the realities they confront. They are ill-treated by the society as their identity, dignity and rights are denied. They are insecure, and physically and psychologically maltreated by the society.

According to Charles Edwin, Director of Ministry Among Eunuchs (Transgenders) argues that their existence and the livelihood is very much threatened due to widespread apprehension and misconception about their human nature. He continues to say, "They are completely rejected by their own families and immediate social groups as soon as their status as transgender is exposed. They are often stigmatized, driven to extreme conditions of life including deprivation, destitution and even suicide as a result of depression. Many of them take to commerical sex work, boot legging and drug running though not wilful indigence" [Charles Edwin "The Church's Response to "Third sex ", *NCCI Review* vol. CXXV, No. 2, (March 2005), P. 36].

As most of the transgenders are involved in sex work, they are susceptible to Sexually Transmitted Infections (STI) like HIV/AIDS. They are also not classifed as male or female, states Charles Edwin, so they are not given voters identity cards, ration cards and passport and thus not considered as citizens (*Ibid.* , P. 35).

The families, society and the Church are to be responsible to uphold the identity, dignity and rights of the transgenders. They need our care, love and support. The families and society and Churches should have a proper focus to recognize them as human persons with equal dignity and right with others. Explorations are to be made to restore and rehabilitate them (especially those who involve in sex work). Government should have measures to uphold their rights on citizens like right to education, health, shelter and employment . It is also important to explore and promote their talents. They should be organized to conscientize them, equip them and to bring them to the mainstream of the society. We need compassion and empathy in order to identify with their struggles. They need liberation from the clutches of dehumanization. It is important also to affirm justice which is central to the kingdom of God.

III. Theological and Ethical Implications to the Gender Issues

God has created the human beings in his own image (Gen 1: 27, 28), so there is no discrimination in the status, dignity and rights of women and men. Jesus' attitude towards women was also beyond any bias. His approach was fair and just towards women which is reflected in his dealing with Samaritan woman (John. 4) and also the woman who was caught in adultery (John . 8). The Pauline approach to women is one of gender-equality and interdependence (Gal. 3: 28), than oppression and subjugation. The prophets were also severely condemning the prejudices against women as they questioned the irresponsible divorce, sexual abuses and violence against women. Bible always has a concern towards the victimized or powerless women (Gen. 21: 16 ff ; Ex. 22: 22;1Sam1:10 ff; Mt. 15 : 21 ff; James 1: 27). Bible is for liberating and empowering women from the clutches of structural injustices and gender disparities.

The gender-injustice is a global phenomenon. The women are striving for their political empowerment, economic equality and fairness in sexual and marital matters. The sex workers and transgenders are also arguing for their identity, dignity and rights. It is important to note that the Christian Churches, the Christian voluntary organizations, the Governmental agencies and other social organizations should play a vital role in order to curb the oppressive forces and to empower women in a holistic sense.

(a) *Political empowerment*

There should be a deliberate attempt from our social structure to make sure the participation of women in the decision-making bodies. Not only the elite women, the non-elite women also should be given fair representation in the political process. The patriarchal structure should undergo revolutionary changes to accept the role and involvement of women.

On the 10th anniversary of the Women Political Empowerment day (24-4-2004) more than 1500 women gathered and made charter of demands which affirm their rights. Following are some of the demands in the chart.

(a) Raise the percentage of reservation for women in the Panchayati Raj Institutions from 33 per cent to 50 per cent and ensure reservation of seats for women in the State Legislative bodies and in the Parliament.

(b) Facilitate women's association at different levels to act as watchdogs and pressure groups.

(c) Provide the rights to land and housing in joint names of spouses and for single, deserted, dalit, tribal devadasi, widowed and battered women, and for those rendered homeless in caste/communal riots and due to displacement.

(d) Implement women component plan (to assure at least 30 per cent of funds/benefits from all development sectors flow to women) through Panchayats (*Social Action* (Jan. - March 2005); P. 51).

The political structure is also so patriarchal or it domesticates women, so the organizing and mobilizing of women is essential to empower them in order to ensure their political rights. In order to have a women-friendly approach, a radical restructuring is needed in political organization and policies. Due importance should be given in the form of representation, positions and rights for the women . The approach to women has to be emancipatory/ liberative than merely welfarism.

Empowerment is needed for women in all areas of life such as social, economic, political and religious. Hilaria Soundari explains political empowerment process as follows: "In this process adequate information and resources has to be made available for women to make their own autonomous decision-making. Empowerment is used to describe a process by which women become conscious of their own situation and organize collectively to gain greater access to public services. The political empowerment indicators considers their basic political rights, role in decision-making bodies of the State and Central Government, representation in policy-making, participation in political campaigning, leadership quality and ability to politicize their problems" (*Dalit Women*, p. 100).

Theology and ethics propose a humanistic and socialistic approach towards the economic and political empowerment of women. All women, especially the marginalized women such as dalit and tribal women are to be given due participation / involvement in the political process. This can be applied in the religious contexts also. The identity, dignity, rights and participation of women are to be ensured, without any gender-bias, in religious contexts. Here the Churches should act as a role model as part of its witness as a community of just women and men. The biblical conccpts like covenant, liberation, Justice, shalom and kingdom of God challenge any inhuman attitudes towards the powerless or victimized. They are against the gender discriminations.

(b) Economic equality

Gender justice is also needed in the economic context. The political and economic empowerment play complimentary role in the quest for gender-justice. Women should have access to economic resources as it is denied by the male-chauvinist society. The patriarchal structure creates a dependence of women on men as they control the properties and holdings. Economic equality is possible through the control over the family resources, national resources, employment and fair wages. There is a gender divide, bias or inequallity in the arena of economics. As the androcentric economics is prevalent in almost all contexts, the women become the victims of economic inequality.

In the Indian context, the condition of the dalit and tribal women are so worse that inequality is found in social, economic and political life. As they are educationally and economically backward, their condition is very pathetic compared to elite or dominant women. It is important to make radical changes in the economic system to favour causes of women. The income-generating resources are to be equally shared with women. There should be equality in employment opportunities and in wage. The gender-biased attitude, perspectives and theories should go and Government should set up free agencies devoid of bureaucrats (as they are corrupt) and politicians (political parties and politicians have their prejudice and partiality) in order to implement the developmental programmes for the women. A thorough conscientization is needed to make aware the women, especially the poor and marginalized women, in order to avail the economic develpomental programmes.

The Christian Church and the society as a whole should challenge the androcentric economics and develop a perspective which would uphold the right and equality of women in income-generating resources. Radical changes have to take place in our attitude and perpectives in order to make our economic structure women - friendly.

(c) Women - sexual and marital issues

The women are to be protected from victimization in the area of sex and marriage. The patriarchal society considers women as an object and sex- tool. Rape, wife- beating, harassment, dowry- deaths and irresponsible divorces are common in the Indian context.

A radical change in attitude and perspectives is needed to have a positive approach towards these issues. Their identity, dignity and rights are to be upheld. Though the laws are enacted to protect the women from violence in the domestic, public and work place situation, the victimization over women continues. Unless the whole society consciously develop a constructive perspective, it is not possible to curb the irresponsible attitude towards women . The male-chauvinistic elements in culture and religion are perpetuated in the whole of society, which has to undergo a radical re-examination and challenge. Their personhood and humanity have to be recognized without any reservation.

The Christian community should be an example and it has responsibility to conscientize the society to develop a responsible and humane approach to women in relation to sex and marital life. Bible condemns the abuse of sex and marital infidelity (Mala. 2 :14 - 15;Mt. 19:1ff; Prov. 5: 1-9). Bible urges the men to love and respect women (Eph . 5: 25, 28-30). The husbands are supposed to nourish the wives and to love, care and support them.

(d) A Response to sex work

Women involved in sex work should be seen as a structural problem. It is victimization of women. The economic problem (e.g. poverty) is largely contributing to this plight of women. There are also forces to kidnap or to deceive them to entrap them for sex work, as it is a profitable business. But there are women who choose this profession as their last resort for their sustenance. Do we condemn the sex work entirely?

The institution of prostitution or sex work was always condemned by the Bible . It is never legitimized. But those who involved in sex work are dealt in an evaluative way by Jesus . Analysing the structure or system which is evil and irresponsible, Jesus was condemning the evil of sex work and giving room for the victim to be restored. This approach was a loving and humane one (John . 8) Jesus also indicated that the transformed sex-worker has a place in the kingdom of God (Mt. 21: 28- 32). Even as we condemn the evil of sex work, it is important to restore them spiritually and socially (rehabilitation). The Churches, the society including the voluntary organization and the Government machinery should involve in their restoration and development. God is compassionate and concerned of the sex workers, so it is important to redeem or liberate them from their plight. The following suggestions are important in relation to them:

(1) The negative attitude towards sex worker should be changed.
(2) Conscientize (eg: moral teaching and counselling) the sex worker about the need of restoration.
(3) Recognize their dignity and identity and rehabilitate them in a constructive manner.
(4) Promote their involvement and use their creativity for the good of the society.
(5) Equip them (e.g: teaching skills) so that they can be given alternative employment.

(e) An approach to transgenders

The transgenders are undergoing severe psychological pressure from the society as their identity and dignity are neglected and they are considered as a curse by parents, relatives and the society. The Churches are also not consciously involved in the liberation of transgenders. The Church and the society do fail to recognize their identity and personhood or to provide care and support to them. Efforts should be made to uphold the identity, dignity and rights of the 'third sex' or 'third gender'.

As most of the transgenders find their identity among sex-workers, what is the responsibility towards them to liberate them ? The document and certificates usually refer only to two genders (Male or Female), and the third gender (transgender) is ignored. The Churches, society and voluntary organizations should organize them and to undergird them . Their status in the society has to be upheld. Their roles and potentialities should be recognized.

Jesus refers to the 'third sex'as those who are born as eunuchs (Matt. 19: 12). God also expresses special concern to the' third sex' (Isa. 56: 3-5). Their identity is recognized and they will be honoured. The Ethiopian eunuch was accepted into the kingdom of God through Philip the evangelist (Act. 8:24-40). There was no reservation to make him a disciple of Jesus Christ (refer, Charles Edwin, Op. Cit. P. 36). We can emphasize the following things:

(1) Their identity or humanhood should be accepted in family, society and Church.

(2) They should be helped to find out employment for livelihood.

(3) They are to be motivated to be active participants in the mainstream of the society and Church.

(4) Evolve programmes for the holistic development of the transgenders. Here the Churches, voluntary organizations and the Government can work together.

As God loves the transgenders, we should also have to love, care and show concern to the transgenders. As they are found alienated and dehumanized, Christians should do their best by uplifting them from their plight. A special attention and care are important to guide them and to restore them as some transgenders are involved in sex work. Those who involved in sex work need the rehabilitation.

Conclusion

Gender-bias is a global phenomenon as most of the societies are patriarchal and oppressive in nature. The gender-prejudices are found in the realm of politics, economics, sexual and marital relations and the transgender issues.

It is found that certain amount of changes are taking place as everyone is aware are of recognizing the identity, dignity and rights of women and transgenders. An attitudinal change and concrete action for their holistic development is inevitable to overcome this crisis. The society, the Church, voluntary organizations, the Government and legal system are to work together in order to safeguard the rights and to emancipate women. The victimization is so grave in the context of the poor, black, dalit and tribal women. The condition of the transgender is very pathetic. Building up a humane society which transcends the gender-bias is essential to affirm their dignity, status and rights in every sphere of our society.

8

Children, God and the World

Children face many problems like child health and safety, education, child poverty, juvenile crime, child neglect and abuse and moral development of children. According to a report around 20 per cent of the children in United States are poor (Marcia J. Bunge. *The Child in Christian thought,* Grand Rapid : Wm. B. Eerdmans Publishing Co; 2001. p. 1). Children are a marginalized or a victimized group as they are effected by poverty, malnutrition, child abuse, war, communalism and ethnic conflicts.

According to the 2006 statistics of UNICEF there are about 2.2 billion children in the world, and among them one billion is living in poverty. 640 million children live without adequate shelter. 400 million children have no access to safe water. 1.2 million children are trafficked each year. 15 million children are orphaned by HIV/ AIDS Worldwide. It is estimated that 1.6 million children are killed in conflict since 1990. Due to conflict or human right violations 20 million children are forced to leave homes. Daily death-toll of children worldwide before their fifth birthday is 29,158. The UN statistics also report that almost 100 million street children and people are inhabited across the globe. According to a UNICEF statistics, out of 500 million disabled people Worldwide, 120 million are children and in developing countries 50 per cent became disabled in the first 15years of life. India has 25 per cent of world's child death. It is also observed that 26,500 children die in the world every day. In every three seconds one child is dying. Almost 16,000 children die every-day from hunger related causes. Two-thirds of the children denied opportunity for primary education are girls.

The children are also facing alienation as their parents migrate to other countries for job. Dan Bilefsky states, "for millions of Romanians, migration has been an economic lifeline. But for 12 years old Stefan Ciurea, the thought of his mother leaving to work as a maid in Italy was worse than death: he hanged himself with a leather horsewhip from the branch of a cherry tree" ("Children left behind suffer strains of migration" *The Hindu,* (February 16, 2009), p. 9). It is estimated that 170,000 Romanian children have one or both parents working abroad. Psychologist Denisa Ionescu observed that children of migrants were at high risk of depression and suffer from feelings of abandonment (*lbid.,* p. 9). In the context of family break up also the children suffer from emotional brunt. It is observed by Prof. Andrew Charlin of Johns Hopkins University that it is difficult for children to adjust to a series of partners who move into and out of their homes (*Deccan Chronicle* (August 8, 2008), p. 28). According to Dr. Vikram Prabhu, if children are reared in stable homes with love and warmth, they will grow up as confident adults (*lbid.*, p. 28).

Millions of children are caught up in a life of violence and Bloodshed. It is observed by Janardhan Roye that these children are abducted, purchased and even handed over by their own families to participate in armed conflicts. He states again that their children are deprived of schooling("Children of conflict" *The Hindu* (young world) (March 31, 2009), p. 2). Children less than five years old used as shields for militants. War leaves children orphaned and homeless, living in fear and uncertainty. Children are suffering from psychological trauma as a result of war experiences.

The condition of girl children are worse in the World-wide situation. Child marriage are common in the Indian context. 22.6 per cent girls married before 16, while 2.6 per cent wedded before 13. Before they turn 18 years, 48.4 per cent married girls have children. The children are not only victims of labour but also several other inhuman aspects. They are disregarded by the society in relation to their rights and, they are sexually abused. The condition of the girl children is still, worse as they are even considered as a'trouble' in the society so they are even killed. They live in very inhuman conditions as they are denied of food and education. Recently also the religious leaders talk about the growing menace of the female foeticide which is a very injustice done against the humanity.

It is estimated that the working children in our country are 44 million. 80, 000 to 100, 000 children are working in Kashmiri carpet industry. It is calculated that about 45,000 children work in match and firework factories in Sivakasi and become victims of exploitation. 92 million children in India exist below the poverty line and they are malnourished (K. C. Abraham (ed), *Cry for Life*, p. 8). The children also work in Hotels, factories and shops in low wages.

The condition of the girl children are more tragic than boy children. They are ill-treated by the family members as their dignity is questioned and they are sexually exploited and also malnourished. The children work over-time in factories and draw very low wages. A number of children including girl children, are rag pickers. Sharmila Joshi states that domestic workers are not fed properly. One eleven year old is given a cup of tea every morning without sugar and her meals are meagre. Malnutrition, hardwork and poor access to medical facilities result in several illness like anaemia, skin infection and stomach cramps (*The Unseen worker*, p. 25).

It is found that migrant children are often sexually abused. Tourists sexually molest these children. Child prostitution is reported to be rampant in Goa. Several minors are used in this act. Most of these children are forcibly brought to "enhance" or "develop" toursim. These are to be curbed as it promotes evil and violating the rights and dignity of children. Indian Consitution (Article 24) prohibits employment of children below 14 years of age in factories and hazardous employment. The children labour (Prohibition and Regulation) Act in 1989 regulates employment of children and totally bans it only in 25 hazardous processes and occupations, including beedi-making, tanning, carpet-weaving and making fire-crackers (*The Unseen Worker,* P-40).

The South Asian Association for Regional Corporation (SAARC) declared a year and Decade of the girl child (1990 and 1991-2000). The Government of India announced a national plan of Action for the girl child, 1991-2000. United Nations Convention on the rights of the child was held on 1989 (it does not specifically mention the girl child). U N's Fourth World Conference on Women (1995) deal with girl child (*Assignment: Giving voice to the unheard,* P. 1). A girl child is internationally defined as a human being below the age of 18.

Infant mortality death is very high in India. UNICEF publication "Glimpses of Girlhood in India"states that about a quarter of the approximately 12 million girls born in India every year do not survive to see their 15th birthday. The health problems, malnutrition, parental bias in Uslampatti, near Madurai where it is found that girl children are poisoned to death because of economic burdens like (dowry) towards girl children are causing their death. It is also observed that girl infants are breastfeed less frequency than boys. There is discrimination in the food allocation to girl child.

About the rights of children, United Nations declaration on human rights Article 25 [x] states, "Motherhood and childhood are entitled to special care and assistance. All children, whether born in or out of wedlock, shall enjoy the same social protection". The UN Convention on Rights of the Child was adopted by the Assembly in 1989 as follows :

(a) The right to survival includes the right to life, the highest attainable standard of health, nutrition and adequate standard of living.
(b) The right to protection which includes freedom from all forms of exploitation, abuse, inhuman or degrading treatment, and neglect including the right to special protection in situation of emergency and armed conflicts.
(c) The right to development which includes right to education, support for early childhood development and care, social security, and the right to leisure, recreation and cultural activities.
(d) The right to participation which includes respect for the view of the child, freedom of expression, access to appropriate information, and freedom of thought, conscience and religion (*Inhuman Rights*, PP. 137-138).

Any discrimination to children in the area of education opportunities and participation, sex, food and freedom of expression are unethical.

The child molestation is a grave issue in the Indian context today. The children are sexually used and abused by the men and women. As already indicated the girl children are the ones widely used in prostitution. A new trend in sexuality is that children (boys and girls) are undergoing molestation. The so-called love towards children is usually referred as paedophilia. In a recent report the paedophiles are found in Goa. (Rashmi Saksena. "sex tourism"(cover story – child prosititutes). *The Week* (August 4, 1996), p. 36) It is noted that paedophiles from

Britain, America, Germany, Australia and the Scandinavian countries are coming to third world countries in the garb of tourists to have sex with girls and boys. (*Ibid.*, P. 36) There are two kinds of paedophilies: the preferential and the situational. "Preferential paedophiles are the ones who have clear yearning for sex with children. Situational abusers prefer an adult partner, but find a childless threatening to their self-esteem". (*Ibid.*, P. 37). It can be noted that there are psychological factors also behind the paedophilia.

The children are used or abused by men and women for their sexual gratification. The parents, the relatives and the tuition teachers are reportedly abusing the boy or girl children. There are cases in which the children are sexually abused till the point of death. (Sunil Solomon Ghazan. *Adults Amuzed But Child Abused*, New Delhi:Navdin Prakashan Kendra, 1995. PP. 22-23)"Today thousands of children keep pouring into the urban cities, either kidnapped, or voluntarily. They enter cities due to broken homes, step mothely treatment meted out to them by parents, due to the sexual abuse by their own fathers. Pregnant teenagers committing suicide, boy being homosexually abused, neighbourhood men and women sexually abusing young and innocent children for the pleasure and amusement,"(*Ibid.*, P. 10). It is observed that there are social and psychological reasons behind sexual offences. The unfulfilled sexual desire is one of the reason for it. There are also reasons like emotional instability and impulsiveness of the person. (Stanton Wheeler. "Sex offence : A sociological critique", *The Sociology of Crime and Delinquency*, edited by Melvin E. Wolfang and *et. al*, Toronto: John Wiley and sons, 1970. p. 628)

Harsh Mander states that millions of children are not protected by parents because of a variety of reasons, as the parents are dead, alcoholic, violent or abusive, or in jail or lost, or have abandoned their children. It is also noted, "The parents may also be themselves destitute, homeless, gravely ill or disabled, and therefore unable to care for their children without support"("The child in need" *The Hindu*, (February 22, 2009) P. 3). He also observes that the child may have no home or no means of subsistence due to riots, natural disasters, war and militant conflict, disabilities and incurable terminal ailments (*Ibid.*, P. 3).

Children are a vulnerable group who are exploited in different ways and are undergoing suffering and margination. Their dignity, identity and rights are denied. Many children are homeless, parentless, and denied of food, education and health-care. Though the Indian Parliament enacted the Child Act in 1960 and Juvenile Justice Act (care and protection of children) in 2000, the children's care and protection are not sufficiently taken care of. So Harsh Mander suggests the formulation of a comprehensive integrated child protection scheme. The World Health Organization (WHO) had started a global school health programme in 1995 in order to develop health habits among children, protect them from diseases, provide nutritious food to them, giving them exercise and counselling. The organizations like 'World vision' and 'Compassion International'are also seriously taking care of the welfare of the children. The food, education and health of children are taken care of.

Marcia J. Bunge observes "In the first place, until very recently, issuues related to children have tended to be marginal in almost every area of contemporary theology. For example, systematic theologians and christian ethicists have said little about children, and they have not regarded serious reflection on children as a high priority"(*The Children in Christian Thought*, P. 3). To an extent it is true that children's concerns were not taken seriously, but now the perspectives are changed.

According to Karl Rahner, children have value and dignity in their own right and are fully human from the beginning. He also recognizes that Jesus uses children as examples of entering the region of God (*Ibid.*, PP. 18-19). In the Biblical perspective children are very valuable and their dignity is affirmed. In Jesu's view they are valuable in the kingdom of God. They are also portrayed as models (Mt 18: 2-5; 19:14; Lk18: 17). The children also glorify God as they are strengthened by Him (Ps. 8:2). It is stated that the historical faith has to be transferred to children (Dt 4 : 9-10) and they are to be cared and properly disciplined (Ps. 119:9; Prov. 22 :6). Children are a valuable gift from God (Ps. 127:3). Children are a great blessing to family (Ps. 127:4; Ps. 128:3, 6) John Calvin and Martin Luther were conscious to providing right condition to raise children in Godliness and the responsibility of civil authorities to provide universal education for both boys and girls (Marcia J. Bunge *op. cit.*, P. 24).

The family, the Church, the society and the Government have their particular responsibility to the bringing up of children. Their value and potentiality are to be recognized and help them to develop, as they are to be responsible citizen and members of the society. They are to be equipped morally, mentally, physically and educationally. The holistic development is necessary in their nurturing. Children are to be protected from structural evil like sexual abuse, child labour and using them in war and drug trafficking. Care should be given to provide them food, shelter, security and support.

9

Caste System/Dalit Issues

Caste system is a hierarchical structure of discrimination developed by Brahminic system. It is an Aryan crude method to dehumanize the Dravidians. The English word 'caste' is derived from the Spanish/Portughese word 'casta'which means race, breed or lineage. According to M. N. Srinivas, caste system is a hereditary endogamous and localized group having a traditional occupation and a definite position in the hierachy of caste. There are different theories behind the origin of caste system. The theories are as follows:

(a) Varna Theory

Caste was developed on the basis of colour in the Vedic period. There was a difference between Arya and Anarya. Brahmin, Kshatrya and Vaisya belonged to Aryavarna. Sudra and Panchamas belonged to the Anarya or Dasavarna. This theory insists the varnashramadharma or caste duty. The Hindu scriptures subscribe the caste system by saying that Brahmins, Kshatryas, Vaisyas and Sudras come out of Brahman's mouth/ head, hands, thighs and feet respectively.

(b) Priestly theory

According to this theory caste system is the creation of the priestly class in order to assert their superiortiy over others.

(c) Functional theory/occupational theory

The differences in occupations has resulted in the caste system. The people who do similar jobs grouped together and formed as guilds and which give form to caste system.

(d) Ritual theory

The purity consciousness in rituals and family meals exclude others and this had led to the development of caste system.

The theories have their own problems. The main question is how the pollution has occurred in caste system. There was a definite attempt by some selfish groups to undermine the dignity and identity of other groups. It is done by either forcing them to do menial jobs, or by considering them as inferior on the basis of colour or by regarding them as impure because of colour and the occupation.

The caste becomes an essential part of Hindu religious tradition. The Aryans claimed that they are the dominant race and subjugate other by the use of force or by misuse of religion. It is interesting to note that Dr. S. Radhakrishnan and Gandhiji equated caste system with class system. They failed to see the dehumanizing elements in caste system. The pollution and discriminiation associated to caste system are evils. Jainism and Buddhism protested the caste system. Dr. B. R. Ambedkar and Jyotirao Phule were strongly challenging the evils of caste system. Caste system is like 'apartheid'. There is a strong element of untouchability in it. Education, employment, access to income generating resources, increasing participation in the socio-political life and furnishing their rights can be the means to help them to come out of their present status of discrimination and indignity. The caste identity should be realized only as a community identity and not as means to underestimate a group of people in the name of birth, colour or occupation. The main problem with caste system is that a person is born with indignity which is a serious discrimination.

Though the Christian principle is not supporting the caste system, the dominant groups try to enslave others and oppress them. The dominant groups controls the Church for accomplishing their interests. The dalits are used by the Church and society for their selfish interests and as vote banks. It is interesting to note that there were separate Churches and cemeteries built in certain places for the dalits to affirm the completion of discrimination.

According to Gandhiji, untouchability is a crime against God and man. Bible states that all human beings are created with equal dignity and no one is to be discriminated (Gen 1:27, 28). Jesus regarded highly the dignity and status of all so-called outcastes like samaritans, lepers, diseased, non-jews and the poor. He loved them and healed them. Apostle Paul also holds a vision that transcends the disparities (Gal 3:28). The Christian community should be an agent of transformation in the society to challenge what is evil. It should also act as models by which others could also follow the path. It is important to know that man is God's creation and he should not be discriminated by any reason.

Dalit emergence

'Dalit'means oppressed, crushed or scattered. They represent the powerless people of India who are the so-called low castes. They are socially, economically and politically alienated. Their rights are denied. In the religious hierarchical order, they are fixed at the end as untouchables. As they are landless and poor they have to depend on the land owners or the dominant caste for their survival. Most of them are bondslaves or born slaves. The Dalit consciousness has emerged and now they try to organize themselves against the oppressive structures. What Bhimrao Ambedkar has dreamt will come true in the near future. The dalits of India can dream of a good future. Of course they can have hopes. As the Blacks of North America sang, the dalits of India also can sing, 'we shall overcome some day'.

So far the dominant classes of India had domesticated the dalits of India. The dalits could only stay under the shadow of the upper caste. The aspiration of the dalits were surrendered to the dominant classes of the India. The voting power of the dalits were manipulated by the oppressive classes. The minorities of India like the Muslims, the Sikhs, the Buddhists, the Jainists, the Christians and the oppressed brethren from the Hindu religion should unite together against Brahminical dominance. The five thousand years of upper caste oppression should go. The dalits of India should join together disregarding the differences for the great target of demolishing the oppressive structure of India.

The dalits were burnt, harassed and prevented from progress (educational, socio-economic and political). The dominant classes have used the dalits as vote-banks and their privileges were usurped. So far the Brahminical dominance has reigned India by manipulating the dalit votes. The dalits have been kept away from the mainstream of the society. The greatest poison that still prevail in the Indian society is none other than the caste system and the resultant exploitation and suppression. The caste system disintegrates, oppresses, dehumanized and departmentalizes the Indian masses. The dalits were considered as sub-human. They were not given any importance than a beast. They were used as slaves. They were tortured. The dominant classes of India had the'privilege'of tapping their labour power and wisdom for their benefit. They never share power and resources to dalits.

The dalits are understood as weak and frail. The emergence of the dalits discloses the fact that no one can be suppressed for a long time. The plight of the dalits will not stay forever. The wind of change is very much visible in the Indian continent. The dalits are acknowledged as a significant power in India today. There was a time when the dalits could not find any meaning in life. They saw the future as dim. But today there is rays of hopes. The dalits should have only one aim, that is to overcome the evil structures which dehumanize them. Paul Lehmann, the American ethicist opined that God is keeping human life human. Yes, the responsibility is to respond to God's act of humanization.

The emergence of the dalits is a watershed in the history of India. The misguided religions and political parties are not the great concern of the dalits, but their liberation as they respond to God's liberative act. They are no longer bound to a Brahminical God who promotes indignity and inequality. God is siding with the dalits, since God is active in history to liberate the oppressed. The evil structures cannot sustain all the time. They may prevail for sometime, but would be eventually defeated. The incarnation (Christ event) is for the deliverance of the poor. Jesus was challenging the oppressive elements and he did work for the liberation of downtrodden and outcaste of the day. The real India can come to existence only through the emancipation of the dalits. India's hopes can be fulfilled only when the aspiration of the dalits is realized. The dalits should have the awareness and self-determination and they all have to work for their emancipation.

Mahatma Gandhi has called the dalits of India as Harijans, the people of God. It is evident that the dalits have traditionally worshipped Siva and not Vishnu or Krishna, so they should be called as Sivajans. Today the dalits belong to different religious communities, but their destiny continues to be the same. Dravidians are the orginal inhabitants of India, but they were suppressed by the Aryan invaders. This suppression and the consequent exploitation and discrimination over dalits continue over centuries. The Brahminical dominance became an unquestionable power in the Indian context. Different communities had competed with one another in order to oppress the dalits. In Kerala also the Christians who claim the Nambuthiri (Kerala Brahmins) tradition and the Syrian tradition also have shown so much of disparity towards the dalits.

Dalits as the oppressed humanity

The Indian society, regardless of Christians and non-Chistians, the caste system is upheld. Rev. Dr. Alphonsus Mathias, the former Archbishop of Bangalore has rightly said in the 'foreword' to the book 'Dalit Christian:A socio-economic Survey' by Ambrose Pinto, "The Scheduled Castes in the country today are in an ambivalent position. Economically, they are the most backward and socially the most retarded. For centuries, they have existed as the most deprived and ostracised people. They have not been permitted to play a significant role in nation-building. Vested interest groups have kept them out in the decision-making process of the country. Any attempt to organize them was looked upon with fear and suspicion by Upper castes and classess".

Caste system is the curse and cancer of Indian Society. The evil of caste system have left no area untouched. It permeates without any reservation. This poison has contributed to socio-economic and political inequality. Because of the centuries long oppression, they are economically retarded, politically weak and psychologically broken. Regret to say that the Churches accepted the Lordship of the dominant class and caste. The status of a dailt as a human being is seriously questioned by the dominant castes. Nobody is here to uplift them and to encourage them. All rights are denied to them. They are not found in the mainstream. Many Churches are oppressing or closing their door to the dalits.

The psychological brokenness is a serious threat. The dalits have found it uneasy to move with the dominant because of their inhuman attitudes. Here the question of integration or separation is also very important. The cruelty of discrimination cannot be tolerated all the time. It is human to challenge the unjust structures. It is Christian to throw away the structures of inhumanity. The Armageddon is not only a final catastrophe, but also a daily experience. The evil and injustice are to be challenged and defeated. Christian message is radical and revolutionary. The mission today is nothing other than conscientizing the dominant castes against the prejudices towards the dalits. Many theologians are fascinated by the Advaita strand of Indian philosophy. While the Vedas and Upanishads have ample references about caste system and its legitimization, how can Advaita be hailed ? The problem in Indian theological sphere is that theology is created by the dominant and for the dominant. Theological integrity is not blind accommodation but challenging the evil and falsehood.

The dalits are down-trodden. They are not found in the mainstream of the society. Though the major part of Indian population constitute the dalits, they have not yet received any recognition. All the crooked ways are used by the powerful to suppress them. In this context the dalits of India regardless of their religious affiliations should unite and organize to gain their rights such as liberty and equality. The dalits have to wake up from their inferiority feeling and rise to consciousness. They should stop surrendering their dignity to the dominant. The dalits are pure race and they are the indigenous people of India. Originally they are Indians. The meaningful co-existence of various communities in India lays its emphasis on equality, fraternity and agapeic love.

The dalits also have to develop the feeling of oneness. The plight of the dalits is none other than their disunity. Unless they are organized, no liberation is possible for them. The educated and the enlightened dalits should try to work for the emancipation of the fellow dalits. They should learn to accept and respect each other. They should realize the urgency of their liberation. It is the duty of the dalits to struggle for their identity and dignity. The different communities should also be enlightened to change their attitude towards the dalits. Socialism, liberty, equality and fraternity cannot prosper in India unless the dailts are uplifted. The transformation and development of India cannot be achieved without the development of the dalits. The dilemma of dalits is the dilemma of India as a nation since dalits are the backbone of India.

The Dalit Christians and Constitutional Rights

The dalits are the oppressed, marginated and voiceless people of India. Anyone who is oppressed is a 'Dalit' in the broad sense of the term. Since the so-called low caste people are oppressed and crushed ruthlessly by the dominant and the term 'dalit' is referred specially in relation to them. They are socially weak, economically backward and politically powerless. The caste system has contributed to the pathetic condition of the dalits. They are, now, away from the mainstream of the society. Historically they were alienated for more than five thousand years. This Dravidian community which is scattered in different parts of India, as a result of Aryan suppression, is struggling to come up.

Around fifteen per cent of the dalits in India are Christians. It is also observed that around three-fourth of the Christians in India are dalits. The dalit Christians are thrice oppressed. They are being oppressed by the society, the Church and the Government. The Simon Commission in 1927 summarized the demands of dalits which includes (1) adequate respresentation for dalits in local, provincial and central legislatures, (2) extension of franchise, (3) safeguarding their education and civil right. Dr. B. R. Ambedkar has considered dalits as a separate minority from Hindu community. The question before Simon Commission was whether Christian dalits should be considered separately or not. The All India Adi- Dravida Jana Sabha argued that the dalit can be a depressed one even after becoming a Christian or after conversion.

It should be asserted that whether Hindu or Christian, dalits are depressed so religion should not be a barrier to consider them as scheduled castes. We find a discrimination in the Constitution itself which goes against the vision of the preamble that affirms the equality, liberty and justice of all, regardless of caste and religion. The articles 14 and 15 of the Constitution do not accept any kinds of discrimination on the ground of religion, race, caste, sex and place of brith.

It is surprising to note that the Government of India Act, 1935 argues that no Indian Christian shall be deemed a member of a scheduled caste. The Constitution has been amended several times to define the scheduled caste. In 1950, the Constitution (Article 314 - which empowered the President to form a list of scheduled castes) explained that only Hindus are scheduled castes and no other. In 1960, it is defined that the Sikhs, the Jainists and Buddhist can also be recognized as 'Hindu' and they should be included in the scheduled caste list. It is interesting to note that our Constitution has recognized that dalit converts to Jainism, Buddhism and Sikhism Hindu, and failed to recognize the dalit converts to Christianity. This discrimination goes against the secularist ideals of our Constitution. What the Christian dalits demand is not to recognize them as Hindus, but to consider them as scheduled castes to have their Constitution rights and privileges.

The dalit Christians are an oppressed group of people along with all other dalits. So they should get their privileges in the area of employment, education and economic assistance which will enhance their social mobility. Whether Christians, Hindus or Sikhs, the dalits are dalits and they are being oppressed. So the dalit Christians also should be Constitutionally protected. In the struggle of the dalit Christian to get their Constitutional privileges, all the dalits should unite. The cause of the dalit Christian is the cause of all dalits. Sad to say, certain Hindu dalit organizations are protesting against the inclusion of dalit Christians in the scheduled caste list. All dalits have to unite in the struggle for their justice. Thanks to the Christian Churches which stand firm for the cause of the dalit Christians.

For a Fair World Order

In the midst of inequality, exploitation and injustice, the subject of a fair World order has its own significance. Inequality has, somehow, become an integral part of our social structure. The dominant class tries to maintain *status quo* so that the programme of exploitation can be continued. Building up of a just society is the pressing need of today. Even the Church as well as the society seem to have ignored the cause of the poor, so their condition remains the same. Unless, the liberation of the poor is a commitment of everybody, the condition of the poor cannot be changed.

The caste system is a psychological, philosophical and

physical oppression. The poor in India mainly belong to the so-called lower castes and they constitute the bulk of our population. Their health and educational facilities are not satisfying. They are oppressed by the dehumanizing social, economical, political and religious system. The instruments of capitalism are regulating all these systems. They live mostly in villages and are alienated from the mainstream of the society.

Even in the matter of medical facilities, the rich enjoy the most sophisticated treatment while the poor have the worst. The poor die without getting proper treatment. According to U. N. universal declaration, "everyone has the right to a standard to living adequate for the health and well being of himself and of his family" (*Health Care in India*, edited by John Desrochers and *et. al* p. 3) Compared to urban areas the rural village facilities are very pathetic. Education is only a dream to the poor. There is lack of motivation and opportunity for them to continue their studies. The facilities available to them are very meagre.

The dalits (Harijans) of India are a sad lot. They are powerless. Most of them are bonded slaves. The Dalits are oppressed and exploited, and are even denied fair wages. They are a Voiceless people. They are not allowed to cross the land and houses of high castes. The temples are parctically closed to them, even now. The water wells are prohibited to them. Their women are harassed and raped and they are asked to keep away from shops. When the dalits are attacked, the police simply close their eyes. They take no action against the assailants. The dominant classes are jealous of their development and educational progress.

It is an irony that the historians of our great nation have really ignored the contribution of the dalits. Their contribution in the independence struggle and their role in social reform is simply forgotten. The Church too has forgotten to record the contribution of the dalits. The police has registered fake cases against them, and there are instances in Kerala and Karnataka that the police is alleged to have forcibly made the dalits eat human excreta. These kinds of dehumanizing acts are taking place in a civilized country like ours.

The violence again the Dalits are increasing everyday. The dalits are disorganized, and the time has come for them to get organized. John Kumar has well portrayed the condition of the dalits in India. He is of the opinion that their per capita income, is not even Rupees two hundred, and many of them go to sleep with empty stomachs. In districts such as Calicut and Wynad, the poor tribals are being deceived by threats and with alcohol, to obtain their land. The History of India is a record of exploitation and systematic violence.

The poor are, after all, suffering everywhere. They are horribly affected by the oppression of the internal and external exploitative elements. The dominant class of the third world countries are evidently joining hands with the multinationals to exploit the poor. Unless man recovers from the sin of selfishness, it is impossible for them to have a fair world order.

The contradiction in our democracy is greatly obvious. India is said to be the largest democratic nation in the world, but it has also degenerated to a large extent. The corrupt bureaucracy of our country has swallowed up most of the developmental programmes and their benefits. They have failed miserably to implement the programmes for the development of the poor. According to Justice, Mr. V. R. Krishna Iyer, there cannot be any democracy without justice. The sorry fact is that corruption has become a part and parcel of our structure, from the top to the bottom. Fairness is absolutely absent. Justice, Mr. Krishna Iyer say again that a casteless classless society was the dream of those who struggled for independence. But it has dashed to despair after we attained Independence.

Tyranny of Ranvir Sena

The dalits have been oppressed by the dominant for many centuries. Now, the dalits are trying to come out of the oppressive forces like the elitistic/ Brahminic dominance and the feudal lords. The dalits are organized to guard themselves from exploitation. The feudal lords/ landowners of our country do not tolerate the emergence of the dalits as a force. So the Ranvir Sena is formed in order to oppress the dalits.

The dalits were treated as slaves, objects, untouchables and inferior beings by the Brahminic class. They forced to do labour for Rs. 10 or 15 per day. Today the situation is changing because of the growing awareness among the dalits. They are conscious of their dignity and rights. The upward mobility and their emergence are understood by the dalits as a threat. So the feudal structure is using violence against dalits in order to oppress them. Ranvir Sena is a banned organization. They have killed 23 dalits in Sankarbega village (23 Jan., 1999) and 12 dalits in Jahanabad (11 Jan., 1999). The Government of Bihar had failed to find out the culprits. The attacks on dalits are continuing. The killing were brutal, ruthless and inhuman. The Ranvir Sena is understood to be formed in order to protect the landords. It is reported that till date they have killed more than 281 poor villagers. It is to be noted that the Ranvir Sena has deliberately used violence against the dalits without any provocation. Few years back they had killed several dalits in Lakshmon badhe.

The Ranvir Sena should realize that they are playing with fire by involving in the inhuman act of killing innocent dalit men, women and children. It is the prime duty of the Government to protect the dalits. It is also important that the dalits should organize themselves to curb the violence of Ranvir Sena. An awareness should be created among the people to identify and to respond creatively to the brutal acts of the Ranvir Sena, the goondas of the feudal powers.

The dalits are the oppressed and marginalized, socially and politically. It is important to realize the need to emancipate the dalits from the clutches of unfreedom, injustice and exploitation. The liberation of India is solely depending on the liberation of the dalits.

10

Tribal Issues

The tribals are the indigenous people who are having a particular geographical area or territory with distinctive culture. They have a particular world view and behaviour pattern and value system. They are the aboriginal people. In India eight pcr cent of the population is tribals. The Red Indians and the Maoris are the aboriginals and there are a number of tribal groups in the East and West. They are mostly the forest-dwellers or 'Vanavasis'. They are the people of the land and the early inhabitants. They live by the forest. They call themselves as the sons of soil. The soil and water are sacred to them. Forest is their main source of food.

In the name of development, the tribals are disturbed. Their habitat is being destroyed. They are considered as the landless people as they have no legal document. They are chased away without having any concern. Their rights are denied and oppressed. They are exploited as their resources are tapped by these forces. Their humanity is not recognized by them. It is important to upold their rights and dignity. The Red Indians of United States and the Maories of Australia are almost annihilated by the Whites for the sake of selfish interests.

In India, the lands of tribals are annexed by the dominant class by force or by deception. Their illiteracy, ignorance and innocency are being exploited to gain their goals. They are economically poor and politically powerless, so it is essential to empower them. In the name of development, making of dams and factories, the tribals are forcefully evacuated. They are made landless and powerless and shelterless. In the name of Narmada valley project (in India), around ten lakh tribals are evacuated and they live without proper living conditions.

The Government authorities are not serious to take care of their food and health. The famine and diseases are common among the tribals. There is illiteracy and malnutrition. As they are paid low wages, they are not able to improve their living condition. They should be given their rights over the land, and also they have to be conscientized as to provide guidance to life. It is important to note that the ecological disturbance adversely affect the tribal people.

(1) The Biblical perspective upholds the rights of the marginated including tribals. Their life is to be safeguarded.

(2) It is the human responsibility to safeguard their land, right and humanity. Never try to disturb their habitat or exploit their resources. The territorial integrity of tribals is to be protected.

(3) The rights of the tribals over the land is to be restored. (In the recent struggles of Kerala Adivasis /tribals under the leadership of C. K. Janu, the Kerala Government had resolved to grant them one to five acres of land). Their privilege should not be grabbed by bureaucracy. It is observed that the term scheduled tribes first appeared in the Constitution of India and article 366 (25) defined it as such tribal communities as are deemed under article 342 (N. K. Vaid, *Who Cares for Tribal Development*, P. 14).

The tribals are denied of their identity, dignity and rights. They belong to 'no people' 'no land' category according to the understanding of Government and dominant class. The territorial integrity and autonomy are the significant factors for the tribals which are being violated. Their humanity is questioned as they are victimized and their women are sexually exploited. It is unfortunate that they are referred as 'uncultured' and 'uncivilized'. Most of the tribals have become landless, bonded labourers. Their privileges are grabbed by the powerful and development is very minimal in the tribal context. Most of the developmental programmes are to tap their resources and to evacuate them forcefully from their habitat. The recent Nandigram, Singur incidents in West Bengal in the name of Special Economic Zone and Tata's Nano project is one of the best example for this.

The first official reference to classify tribals was found in Government of India Act, 1935 where it is referred 'Backward tribals'. After the existence of Constitution in 1950, the classfication of scheduled castes and tribes was made, states Lalrinawmi Ralte [*Religion and Society*, vol. 50 (Sept. 2005), P. 25]. According to N. K. Vaid, "The Constitution of India does not define Scheduled Tribes as such. Article 366 (25) refers to scheduled tribes as those communities who are scheduled in accordance with Aritcle 342 of the Constitution. This article says that only those communities who have been declared as such by the President, through an initial public notification will be considered as "Scheduled Tribes". (*Who Cares for Tribal Development.* New Delhi : Mittal Publications, 2004. P. 5). The Lokur Committee has identified Scheduled Tribes having following characteristics.

> (a) Primitive traits (b) Distinctive culture, shyness of contact with public at large, (c) Geographic isolation, (d) Social and economic backwardness (*Ibid.,* P. 6).

According to 1991 census, the tribal population in the country is 67.76 million constituting 8.08 per cent of the total population. The literacy rate among them is 29.6 per cent and female literacy among tribals is 18.2 per cent. It falls below the overall literacy rate of the country (52.2 per cent). The Constitution of India guarantees equality in the form of provisions for the advancement of tribals [Article 15 (4)], in matters of appoinment to any office under the state (Act. 16) and in matters of promotion [16 (4 A)]. They are protected from social injustices and exploitation and State is giving special care in their educational and economic interests (Act.46). Politically, the tribals are having reservation seats in the Parliament (Art. 330), Legislative Assemblies of the states (Art. 332) and in Panchayat (Art. 243 D). The Ministry of Tribal Affairs is constituted in October 1999 for the justice, development and empowerment of tribals (*Ibid.*, PP. 12 - 13).

According to Nirmal Minz the colonial British attitude was not able to appreciate the tribal values. He states "The communitarian ownership of properties, equality among people, democratic organizations and decision by consensus in the administration of law and order, accomodative spirit and the acceptance of all human beings with hospitality, honesty and truthfulness, among the tribal people in India were not accepted as human values by the colonial Government and even by our National Government in our country" ["Tribal Issues in India today" *Religion and Society* vol. 50, No. 3 (Sept. 2005), PP. 6-7].

Nirmal Minz, continues to opine that the Government of India has officially denied the existence of indigenous tribal people in India and Government of India do not want the Adivasis to continue as a distinct people in this country (*Ibid.*, P. 8). Government of India and also some Sociological theorists like G. S. Ghurye, he states, who are looking forward the assimilation of the tribals into the mainstream of the society (*Ibid.*, P. 8). These are the threatening situation of the identity of the tribal people as they are objectifying and dehumanizing tendencies. The Indian Government and society should not nullify the emergence and empowerment of the tribals. Their future has to be bright as they live as a people with identity, dignity and rights. Sangh *parivar* does like to refer tribals as Vanavasis (Forest-dwellers) than Adivasis (original inhabitants) in order to reduce the Adivasis to a people without a history, states Santanu Patro (*Religion and Society,* vol. 50, Sept. 2005, P. 12). This is also a threat to their identity and status. The fundamentalism and pseudo secularism which insist on a single religion, culture and ideology is also a threat to the pluralistic foundation of our nation and to the identity of Dalits and Adivasis. It reduces the religious minorities, dalits and Adivasis as second class citizens (*Ibid.*, P. 17).

The Sangh *parivar* will also deny the identity, dignity and rights of minorities and subaltern groups. Hinduism is used by brahminic forces and Sangh *parivar* as an umbrella under which they nurture caste system or Varnashramadharma to uphold their dominance. The recent incidents (2008) in Orissa, the Sangh *parivar* used tribals against Christian tribals for their interest.

The land is life for the tribals which is robbed from them by the British colonizers, the zamindars and other dominant communities. They also became landless as the land is taken by force or evacuated them from it by the Government authorities. The land is lost and become landless labourers. The immigrants also grabbed the tribal land by deceptive means. According to P. Alexendar, they are also exploited by the selfish traders and greedy money-lenders(*Ibid.*, P. 42). They had to surrender their properties and land for their loans to these people. The triblas are also forced to become bonded labourers (*Ibid.*, P. 43).

It is the responsibility of the Church, society,

Government and voluntary organizations to work for the development and liberation of the tribals. These sincere people should be protected from social, economic, political and sexual exploitation. Politically, they have to be brought to the mainstream of the society by ensuring their participation in decision-making. They should be considered with justice.

God is just and Bible stands for the liberation of the marginalized. The identity, dignity, rights and liberation of the victimized or the subatern is upheld by the Bible (Ex. 3:7, 10) Israelites were the tribal group who were oppressed and exploited by Egyptians, where God responds to their cry and liberated them. God does have solidarity with the poor, aliens and those who cry for their identity, dignity and rights (Isa. 58: 6- 7; Am. 5:12, 24; Lk. 4: 16 - 21). The conscientization and mobilization of the tribals is important to gain their rights. The different kinds of exploitation by immigrants, bureaucracy and the landlords have to be stopped.

11

Poverty, the Plight of the People

One of the worst enemy of humanity is the poverty. It is a fierce demon which makes the life of the people miserable. Millions of people on this earth are affected by the extreme poverty. Poverty is the fate of many in the context of prosperity. Many are dying everyday because of poverty. In the context of war, ethnic violence, communalism, population explosion and natural calamities the poverty would be increased.

Poverty is a major issue in the Third World. One of the main causes of poverty is the exploitation. The oppressive spirits tried to accumulate the resources by all means and they leave a major group of people marginated. The capitalistic and feudal socio-economic structures so also colonialism contribute to poverty. The Asian and Latin American countries have suffered a lot from colonialism. The elites of the Third World and the colonizers gained much by their exploitation.

Poverty are of two kinds- absolute poverty and relative poverty. The absolute poverty is worse that the poor could only live by absolute dependence on others. Those who are in relative poverty are relatively in better position. The poverty becomes worse in the context of war and communalism. Many die of food, the poor cannot survive with dignity. The unemployment is also a significant cause for poverty. People die because of starvation as there is no proper supply of food, or adequate distribution of food.

The Third World context is poverty-stricken. The poverty deaths are not uncommon in the Third World countries. The poverty has caused malnutrition which, in turn, contribute to different diseases such as tuberculosis, anaemia, fatigue, ultimately the premature death. It is observed that half of the World's population is malnourished. Many children also die before they reach their teens because of extreme poverty. Most of the poor live in huts as there is no proper shelter. They fail to send their children to education as there is no sound economic background.

Most of the poor live in gettoes. They are the slum-dwellers, where there is no basic facilities. They live in unhygienic situations, so contagious diseases are common. The brain damage caused by protein deficiency and infant mortality rate is high among the poor. According to Ronald J. Sider, proverty means hunger, illiteracy, disease, brain damage and death. Ronald Sider narrates the story of Iracema Da Silva, resident of slum in Brazil. In the extreme situation of poverty, Iracema said "sometimes I think, if I die, I won't have to see my children suffering as they are. Sometimes I even think of killing myself. So often I see them crying, hungry; and there I am, without a cent to buy them some bread. I think "my God, I can't face it I'll end my life. I don't want to look any more" (*Rich Christians in an age of hunger* P. 17). This instance depicts the stark reality of poverty which leads people to 'death'.

In the Indian situation more than 60 per cent of the people are poor. It is calculated that around 40 per cent of the people live below the poverty line. They suffer from unemployment, malnutrition and lack of food and shelter. They go to bed with a single meal in a day, with a square meal or without any meal. Even after eight to ten hours hard work they earn only 10 or 15 rupees a day. Most of them are bond-slaves or unorganized workers, so justice and proper wages are denied to them.

What is Poverty?

Poverty is the state where people live below the subsistence level. The food, shelter and the employment are essential for the dignified existence of man. In India, around 40 per cent of the population live below the poverty line. Most of them are going to bed without a meal or with a square meal. Poverty is the situation by which one is not having enough income to have sufficient food, shelter and to have education and health. It is reported that in every minutes 12 children, below 5 years of age, are dying because of starvation. According to Government reports 1999-2000, the percentage of people below poverty line in India is 26.10 per cent nation-wide. But this could be more. There are 1300 million poor in the world.

Most of the poor live in ghettoes or slum, the most unhygienic conditions. The slums are ever increasing in the Indian context as the poor are migrating to the cities to seek food and employment. The slum symbolizes the massive poverty. It is estimated that around 25 per cent of the Indian population is in slums. They have no possibility for a dignified existence (Godwin Shiri, *Our Slums: Mirror a Systemic Malady*, Bangalore:ATC, 1999. P. 1). In each city 500 to 700 slums exist which reflects the gravity of the problem. The poor are struggling for 'Roti; (food);Naukari' (employment) and 'makan' (shelter).

Poverty line is explaind as follows. The minimum required consumption expenditure level of items such as food, clothing, shelter, transport and health-care, which meets the average per capita daily calorie requirement of 2400 calories in rural areas and 2100 calories in urban areas, along with a minimum of non-food expenditure. In 1979, the Planning Commission's task force worked out the monetary equivalents of these 100 ms at Rs. 49.9 per capita per month in rural areas and Rs. 56. 64 per capita per month in urban areas (Manorma Year Book 2002, Kottayam: Malayala Manorama 2002, p. 566).

It is found as explained that Poverty-line is defined in terms of the minimum number of calories (around 2400) required for a human being to live and do ordinary work. This does not include other subsistence requirements like housing, clothing, health and education (*J. Murickan ed. Poverty in India: Challenges and Responses,* Trivandrum:The Xavier Board of Higher Education in India, 1988, p. 41).

According to T. G. Godard, Poverty is an insufficient supply of those things which are requisite for an individual to maintain himself and those dependents upon him in health and vigour. In the words of Gillin and Gillin, poverty is the condition in which a person, either because of inadequate income or unwise expenditures, does not maintain a scale of living high enough to provide for his physical and mental efficiency and to enable him and his natural depending to the standards of the society of which he is a member (K. Singh, *Problems of Sociology*, Lucknow: Prakashan Kendra, 1991, p. 289). For Malthus, growth of population is the cause of poverty, but Karl Marx observes that exploitation is the main source of poverty.

The population is increasing in each second. The world population has reached around 600 crores. India has crossed 100 crores. Thomas Robert Malthus (1766-1834) is considered as the father of population study. He was a Minister of the Church of England and Professor of History and Economics at Cambridge University. According to him, the population is regulated by passion for sex. He suggested certain means to control population growth. The important one is the reduction of birth rate. This is done by (1) a total abstention of marriage, (2) a prudential postponement of marriage, and (3) a voluntary abstinence within marrige.

He was advocating only voluntary abstinence by couples and no means of brith control. He also sees the poverty, famine, pestilence, war and malnutrition as the way in which there is increase of death rate to reduce population growth (Paul J. Koola, *Population and Manipulation*, Bangalore : A. T. C. Publications, 1979, pp. 10-11). His theory is based on his understanding on natural law.

The Structure of Poverty

The poverty is contributed by the structural problems. The unequal distribution of land or income generating resources and the unequal distribution of food and resources are some of the important causes for the poverty. The accumulation of wealth by few is found among the capitalistic structures. In the context of Globalization in modern times, the Multinational Corporations, Transnational Corporations, World Bank and International Monetary Fund are playing key roles to structural adjustment programme which is part of New Economic Policy and the Global cheap labour economy. Globalization promotes disintegration as it widens the gulf between rich and entertained efficiency and competition. It promotes neo-colonialism so entertained exploitation and oppression. It negates the kingdom values-love, justice and shalom (well being of all).

The competition and efficiency are considered as important factors in the globalized context. Here the lion's share of the population are sidelined. They would be found powerless and away from the mainstream of the society. The exploitation, oppressions and different kinds of injustice contribute to poverty. Lack of fair wages and reduction in the employment opportunities also contribute to poverty. The free market economy badly affects the internal economic system of any country as it brings crises in the field of agriculture and industry. The product that is dumped by the foreign forces into the market damage the domestic economy of countries, especially Third World countries.

The Western colonialism had tapped the resources of Third World countries and left the people as poor. The neo-colonialism breaks down the domestic economy of Third World countries by tricks and force. The Asian, Latin American and the African countries are much affected by the neo-colonialism. In order to make an economic crisis, the Westerners exported their goods to the Third World market as part of free-trade. As a result the domestic industry, agriculture and cattle-rearing are adversely affected which also contribute to poverty. The Somalian famine and Rwandan crisis are created by the neo-colonial powers (Michel Chossudovsky, *The Globalization of Poverty,* New Delhi: Madhyam Books, 1977, PP. 76 ff; 101 ff; 111ff).

Response to Poverty

In the context of extreme poverty, all religious traditions and secular ideologies should come together to help humanity to overcome this plight as care and concern should be shown to the marginated and poor. God is the friend of the poor (Deenabandhu). He hates violence (*himsa*) in the form of exploitation. Alleviation of poverty is the responsibility of each person as they should share and contribute to the welfare of the other.

The family planning is very important to control population growth. 'We are one, we have one' is the slogan today. The nuclear families are being developed in the place of extended families. There should be a control of birth rate. This is done, positively to take care of the welfare of the parents and children. The artificial means of birth control are suggested (contraception and sterilization) to regulate the population growth. There is a wide conscientization programme in this regard. It is important to note that the force should not be used in this matter. It should be a voluntary decision of the family.

The Church should also teach the families for responsible parenthood and family planning. Control of birth is not sin. The human beings are given wisdom to act responsibly in the context. This can be applied in the situation of population explosion. Though food is entrusted by God for the need of the whole people, it is controlled by few, so there is no proper distribution. When there is no proper distribution and availability of food, it can lead to malnutrition or death.

The population growth can also result in issue of space, land and shelter. These issues are real. But it should be kept in mind that there is enough space for the people to survive if we avoid the vested interests. The possessive nature of man controls vast amount of food, land and other assets for their own welfare or selfish interests. Though population growth may affect the issue of poverty, it should not be exaggerated. There are several other structural problems (e.g. Feudal system) that lead to poverty.

Right to food and shelter are the basic rights of human beings. M. M. Thomas, the theologian, has referred this as the right to bread. The'anawim'(Hebrew word for poor) and 'ptokos'(Greek word for poor) represent the widows, oppressed and the helpless ones. They depend on other for their survival. They also include the slaves, orphans and sojourners (Zc. 7: 9-10; James 1:27; Lev. 19:10; Ex. 22:21-22). They are the debtors and the landless. The Biblical insights uphold the sharing of resources, safeguarding the welfare and justice to the poor. It challenges the feudal structure that promote poverty (LK. 4:16-21; MK. 12:41-44; LK. 19:1-10; Amos. 5:11;5:5;4:4-5).

In the situation of poverty, it is important to discuss the Christian response. If our neighbour is in poverty or hunger, we should act responsibly, otherwise we are the worst sinners. Live in affluence or luxury is sin, when our neighbours are in utter poverty. According to Nicholas Berdyaev, ' our food is a material problem, and our neighbours food is a spiritual problem'. What measures we could take to respond to poverty ?

(1) Conscientize the dominant class to share their resources.
(2) Church and society should work for a structural transformation.
(3) Church and society has to involve in the development programmes.
(4) Church should challenge the unjust structures in order to have a proper distribution of resources.
(5) Church should form as a responsible community in order to serve in a holistic way to bring changes in the life of the people.

The Churches should unite to resolve the issues of poverty. Strategies and economic policies are to be developed to confront the situation of poverty. Sharing the resources, involving in rehabilitation and development, creating the empolyment opportunities, and protesting against the exploitative structures are important to deal with the issue of poverty. The rich held the lion's share of the resources which should be released for the benefit of the poor.

12

Perspectives on the Issue of Labour

One of the major area of labour is agricultural sector. Most of the Indian villagers work in the field of Agriculture. They are mostly unorganized and getting only a small amount as their wage or payment. They get a maximum of Rupees ten to forty per day. Since they cannot survive with this amount, they become the debtors to the landlords and become slaves to them for centuries. They are unorganized so their rights are denied. A big number of them are also landless and unemployed. Most of the workers are also belonging to the dalit or tribal background. There are substantial number of women also work in the poorly paid sectors. A number of men and women work in the unorganized industrial sector also are lowly paid temporary workers. Their labour force is exploited and not given the benefits due to them.

The dominant class controls the income-generating resources and the marginated groups function as workers or labourers. In the agricultural and industrial sectors there are organized and non-organized labourers. Most of the labours work for daily wages and they do not enjoy any other privileges. There are also bonded labourers who are slaves of the landowners because of the debt. The people work in different sectors. They are working in agricultural sectors, industrial enterprises, fishing sector or even in small-scale industries. The capitalists are controlling the property and resources and the poor are employed by them for mean wages. The extreme poverty, unemployment, malnutrition and epidemics are common among the poor workers.

The divison of labour on the basis of caste and gender is an issue in the Indian context. Especially in rural setup, caste-wise occupation only is possible. This has curtailed their upward mobility. The contract labour is a means of exploitation as they are given low wages and no benefits or rights.

The exploitation and oppression are very high in the Indian structure, as the *Janmis* or landlords are having hectares of land and other income-generating resources and the poor are living as slaves. The labourers are used by the 'Babus' or landlords without giving them proper wages and facilities. The landlords use violence over the labourers as they are considered as objects. Following are the conditions of unrecognized workers.

1. No adequate wages
2. No guarantee for employment
3. No proper shelter
4. Mistreatment, especially to the women workers
5. The practice of slavery.

Equal pay for equal work is insisted by some countries, including United States and India. But it does not work in the unorganized sector as the exploitation continues in this sector and the women are victimized. The cheap labour policy of globalization is also a means of exploitation which affects the marginalized groups as profit is the only aim of the capitalists. Marx and Engels were protesting against exploitation of the labourers in the context of industrialisation in Europe. The right to dignity and wages is as important as right to employment.

In Indian context, there is division of labour on the basis of caste system. The so-called low castes or dalits are insisted on doing the mean jobs and their rights are denied. They are even forced to carry the carcasses. The dailt women are to work as manual scavengers to clear excreta from the houses and offices. Though it is punishable under law, it is still continuing. According to Harsh Mander, "It involves entrapping women, men and even children only because of the accident of the birth into a hatred and humiliating vocation of gathering human excreta from individual or community dry toilets with bare hands, brooms or metal crapers into wicker baskets or buckets" ("Scavenging dignity" *Hindu* (Sunday Magazine) June 29; 2008. P. 3). In 1976, section 7A was introduced into the protection of Civil Rights Act, 1955 to make it an offense, and only in 1993, Parliament to pass the employment of manual scavengers and construction of Dry Latrines (Prohibition) Act, which make manual scavenging an offense. It was found that 95 per cent of manual scavengers are dalits and it is esstimated that six lakh manual scavengers are employed by various private and public bodies (*Ibid.*, P. 3). Though no one is willing to do this work, they are forced to do so because of unemployment and utter poverty. Their dignity in the society is questioned, so they are to be rehabilitated. The Government and their agencies are not effective in eradica-ting manual scavenging.

Exploitation, especially of the women workers, is a common factor in the area of labours. It is reported that in India, out of the 18 million urban women workers, six million are employed in the leather, garments, or textile industries. Because of the economic tsunami or depression, they are even forced to work for Rs. 20 for a 12 hour work day (Brinda Karat, "A century later the issues are very similar" *The Hindu*, March 8, 2009. P. 10).

It is also observed by Mukul Sharma, "The right to

work and rights at work have been heavily curtailed in India in the recent past. And the blame for denial of these rights frequently lies with not only Government but also individuals, groups and enterprises. Defending and promoting jobs, employment and work should be an urgent priority for the Government, the national community, the people movement and civil society as a whole. Nothing can take precedence over the right to work and live with dignity" ["Right to work and rights at work" *(The Hindu* (February 27, 2009). P. 10].

Many fundamental aspects of labour are missing today. Mukul Sharma states, "Fundamental rights at work– elimination of forced and compulsory labour in all its form, equal pay for women and men for work of equal value, freedom of association and ban on child labour – are missing. The right of access to employment without discrimination, free choice of employment, and access to employment which includes appropriate vocational education, rights to fair wages, safe and healthy working conditions, prohibition of dismissal on dubious grounds and equality of treatment in employment are less valued. We seriously lack a basic framework for protection of labour rights and an enabling rights-based environment for equality and development (*Ibid.,* P. 10).

Though article 24 of the Indian Constitution states, "No child below the age of fourteen years shall be employed to work in any factory or mine engaged in any other hazardous employment". The child labour continues in many sectors. According to the observations of Neera Burra, there are four kinds of child labour.

(1) Those children who work in factories, workshops and mines

(2) Those children who are under bondage to their employers, whether in agriculture or industry

(3) Street children - those who live on and off the streets.

(4) Children who work as part of family labour in all context of agriculture, industry home- based work etc. (*Born to Work*, Calcutta: OUP, 1998. P. 11).

1981 census reveals that there are 263 million children aged fourteen years or under in India comprising 39.5 per cent of the total population of the country. Among them 11.2 million are involved in full-time economic activity (Main workers) and 2.4 million in part-time work (marginal workers) (*Ibid.*, P. 11).

It is also estimated that 218 million children in the world engage in child labour. Out of which 150 million are working in the field of agriculture where they are exposed to scorching heat and toxic pesticides. These children are curtailed from education, health facilities, physical and mental development, the rights and dignity. They are exploited and oppressed. Children are even becoming bonded labourers and slaves. They are compelled to become soldiers in the context of armed conflict (It is found in Angola, Burma, Columbia, Congo, Sudan and Uganda). The children, including girl children are trafficked for labour exploitation and sexual abuse. Trafficking of children to tourist centres for sexual abuse is a tragic element. They are infected by diseases and even HIV/AIDS. These kinds of cases are found also in Goa and Kerala.

The child labour is a major problem in the Indian situation. It is a cheap labour. They are widely used in hotels and dangerous industrial situations. It is calculated that around forty four million working children in our country. 80,000 to 100,000 children are estimated to be working in the Kashmiri carpet industry, their ages ranging between six to fourteen, working for ten to twelve hours per day, each one earns an amount of Rs. 60 per month. 10,000 children are reported to be working in the wood carving industry in Uttar Pradesh, earning Rs. 10 per day for 14 hours of work. Thousands of children work in the dangerous production of brassware and lock making in Aligarh. About 45,000 children working in Match and Fireworks factories in Sivakasi are also victims of exploitation apart from being susceptible to severe health hazards - from accidents to excessive strain on the lung, arms and shoulders (*Cry for Life* edited by K. C. Abraham, P. 8).

In the Agarbatti units also the children are used. The minimum wages is not given. There is also no protection from the health problem. It is a hazardous work which can cause headache, backache, cough and continuous illness. Though there is a Child Labour (Prohibition and Regulation) Act of 1986, there is no proper measures taken to curb the exploitation.

The girl children also work in pearl factories which is hazardous. There are also girl children among rag- pickers. The malnutrition, headaches, scabies, asthma, tuberculosis and diarrhoea are common among them (*The Unseen Worker*, P. 10ff).

Bible does not go against the labour. According to Bastian Wielenga, work is understood as an essential part of life (Ex 20:9;2Thess. 3:10). He continued to say, "when Simon the fisherman complains" "Master, we toiled all night and took nothing Jesus directs him to an abundant catch" (*Biblical Perspectives on Labour*, Arasaradi: TTS, 1982. P. 36).

According to Wielenga, "The Bible points out that making a living is not the purpose of life. Life is more than labour and society should be organized in such a way that everybody can enjoy and celebrate the gift of life. That is part of the meaning of the sabbath the seventh day of rest. There should be time for the celebration of the life which we have received. Resting from our work, free before God, we re-disover the purpose of creation and we learn to re-orient our life and work within the framework of God's history with mankind" (*Ibid.,* P. 36). The oppressive masters are challenged as God was identifying with the oppressed working class in Egypt and they were liberated (Ex. 12). God listens to the cry of the labourers and vindicated justice (Ex. 20:2). Jesus offers comfort and rest to the working class (Mt. 11:28). Jesus was always having solidarity with the working class and the powerless (LK. 4: 16 -21). He did sense the suffering of the poor labour class. Jesus and prophets urges the feudal lords to have a fair dealing with the poor and they also look forward a new society which is socialistic in nature. Kingdom of God stands for peace and justice and it questions exploitation.

It is important to accept the identity, dignity and right of the labourers. They should be given fair wages, whether men or women. The child labour is a crime against them so it should be condemned. The labour power of the children should not be exploited. The labour class should get the fair wages, the fair dealing from the authorities and proper dispensing of privileges. The women workers have to be treated with dignity. Equal pay for equal work has to be practiced in private and public sectors.

13

Perspective on Land/Property

There are common properties which are owned by public or the Government. It is either owned by the group or by Government. The land can be also owned by persons, groups or by the Government. Land in India is mostly owned by individuals. The forest area is in control of the Government. Most of the dalit are tenants of the rich landlords and the tribals are the forest-dwellers. They are landless bond labourers.

Land is the main income-generating resource. Land is life for the subaltern people. The nomads become semi-nomads and they later settle in land. The whole World was a 'no man's land' for sometimes. Now people occupy the land and accumulate the land, so the struggle for land also began. The pastoral or agrarian community look for fertile land. In order to occupy the land the different groups used force and other tricks. The Aryans used force and psychological war (tried to establish their racial superiority and claim over Dravidians) against Dravidians. In Australia and United States, the Whites annihilated the Maoris and Red Indians, the original inhabitants of the land. At present the land is alien to these aboriginal groups. It is also happened in India and elsewhere that the dailts and tribals are evacuated by force from their habitant in the name of development. In the Indian context, ninety per cent of the people hold only ten per cent of the land

and other assets. The land is with the landowners. They keep several hectares for their well being. Indian feudal or capitalistic structure make most of the people slaves.

Those who holds the land have wealth or money, and they will have also the power. The rural poor of India are the agricultural labourers and are landless that they are the bond slaves of the landowners or Janmis. The conditions of these bond slaves is that no land, no property, but only poverty. The Indian structure is so capital intensive that the poor cannot come up. It uses all its force to suppress them.

It is to be noted that unless the land and other resources are properly distributed, the poor cannot attain their liberation. Professor Irfan Habib points out the four agrarian classes developed under Mughals:

(1) The Zamindars, moneylenders and merchants
(2) Rich peasants
(3) Middle and poor peasants
(4) Landless labourers who represent low castes and untouchables (*Agrarian System of Mughal India*, PP. 120-121; quoted in *An Ethical Critique of Land Reform* by J. Lawrence, P. 10).

The Indian situation is not yet changed much from the Mughal period. In the urban and rural India, the land and resources are with the dominant groups and others are undergoing severe struggles to survive.

A fair distribution of the land and resources are very essential for a social revolution in India or in any country. The Bhoodan Movement of Vinoba Bhave was contributing to an extent to distribute the land to the landless. Through the Land Reforms Act of 1969, landless of Kerala State obtained a minimum of five cents. Structural change was taking place to an extent through these ways, but they are not quite adequate to bring a radical change in the society.

Land issues are very crucial today as it leads to conflicts and even war. The Indo-Pakistan and Israeli- Palestinian conflicts are the consequences of the issue of land. According to Biblical view, land in God's and human beings are only stewards. It is instructed that the land has to be returned to the owner in the year of jubilee. The slave is to be freed. The land and persons cannot be kept under someone's custody for long. The wealth is always asked to be shared. This is a very clear teaching of Old Testament and New Testament. Oppression or exploitation is never permitted. Jesus admonished the rich to share the resources for the welfare of the poor. It is not mere charity that Bible look forward, but an egalitarian society. The concepts like Koinonia, Jubilee and Liberation are asserting this fact.

The property is the asset, and it can be found in the form of land, building, silver, gold, money or animals. The property can be individual, private, public and common. An individual can own property, so also person and group can own property which is personal and private. The individuals hold property which is individual property. The individual (person) or groups hold property which is private in nature. The public property is the property of the people or society. It is everyone's property but is controlled by Government or boards or public organizations.

The common property can include rivers, oceans and forests. These are the property of all, but is regulated by the Government. They are the common resources. There is also a view that ' common' village lands which is used for grazing, fuel and fodder production. There is also an understanding that individual property should give way to common property. This is a socialistic outlook that this common property should be administered by state. So it insists that property has to be transferred from individual to community. The forests are orginally inhabited by aboriginals, so they cannot be chased away by any forces. They have the right in the land.

There are land struggles in some parts of a country as the dalits and tribals are for their rights on land. The tribals and dalits had land struggle in Wynad (Kerala) in Chengara (Pathanamthitta district, Kerala) and in the area of Narmada Valley project. As the West Bengal Government evacuated the people from Nandigram (for chemical factory) and Singur (Nano project) in the name of Special Economic Zone (SEZ) they protested and succeeded in recovering the land. Forcefully acquiring the land and evacuating the people is a common scene in the Indian context. The people's rights and land is usually denied as they are severely powerless. The marginated groups are severely suffering because of this unfair dealings.

The Indian paradox is that 90% of the income-generating resources are possessed by 10% rich, and 10% of the income-generating resources only is held by the 90% people. This shows the pathetic condition of the poor and powerless. Many people are landless and shelterless. The land mafia is also playing a deceptive role to raise the price of the land, so the poor has no access to land. There should be a proper distribution of land, property and other resources taking into consideration the marginalized. A liberative process is essential in order to fulfil this task. The feudal socio-economic structure has to be radically re-structured for this purpose. Bible stands for the rights to land and other income-generating resources by the poor and marginalized.

Abraham had the promise of the land, which is a divine gift (Gen. 12; Ex. 9:5). God likes to provide the necessary space for the persons and communities to stay on this earth. The fundamental principle among Israelites, according to Chris Wright, is that the land was intended to be equitably shared out, so that every household had its part in the national inheritance (*Living as People of God,* Leicester:IVP, 1983. p. 54). Naboth's inheritance was forcibly taken by King Ahab (1King. 21: 11-16) which was a violation on the right to land and God did punish that injustice. The feudal structure was grabbing the land from the powerless and was never willing to share land and other resources. The jubilee was instituted by God for the renewal and restoration of the land (Lev. 25). Economic exploitation is a crime against humanity. Chris Wright observes that God as creator is Lord and ultimate owner of all created things (*Ibid.,* P. 67). The land and other resources are owned by God (Ps. 24:1), so man's ownership is only subordinate, relative and secondary to God's ownership (*Ibid.*, P. 68).

14

The Slum Dwellers and their Crises

A large number of people all over the world find refuge in slum as they fail to find a space for shelter anywhere. Millions of people in different countries live in ghettoes. The poor in the world are destined to live in slums as they have no regular income or shelter. The film 'slum-dog millionaire' portrays the life of the people in the slum in Bombay, but the dark picture of the slum. The slum reflects the real India, the stark reality of the people of India, as it is quite pathetic.

The evolution of slums

It is noted that there are around 700 slums in Bangalore. India's largest slum is Dharavi (Bombay) which has 4,00,000 inhabitants. Around 50 per cent of the city population is slum-dwellers. According to 2001 census, Tamilnadu has the third largest number of cities and towns with slum population of 63 per cent after Uttar Pradesh (69 per cent) and Andhra Pradesh (77%). The capital city of Tamilnadu, Chennai has more than 1000 slums.

The poor and the migrants find shelter in slums as they do not find a space for shelter in the cities. Slums are found in the posh areas where the women and girl children serve as maid servants in the houses of the rich. Many people, because of poverty and unemployment migrate to cities and find refuge in slums. Those who run away from home, the deserted ones and orphans find space in the cities in slums. The development of the slums is necessitated because of the rush to the cities and the resultant space problem. Only the rich are able to live in flats and villas, the poor roam around in bus stations, railway station and may find refuge in slums.

The word slum in derived from the Greek word 'schlamm' means slime or mud. The Latin 'Labi' is related to this term which means side, slips and sink. The slum is understood as a ghetto or congested area which is an unhygienic, indignified, overcrowded, unsanitary and poor living condition. Poverty, inadequate facilities, unemployment, illiteracy, ill-health and disorganization are the marks of a slum. Slum-dwellers are powerless and live in highly dehumanized situation. Those who dwell in ghettoes are denied of their identity, dignity, rights and privileges.

The slum is described as, "Densely populated area of standard housing, usually in a city, characterized by unsanitary condition and social disorganization", (*Britannica Ready Reference Encyclopaedia*, New Delhi, Encyclopaedia Britannica (India) Pvt. Ltd and Impulse Marketing, 2004. P. 77). It is observed that the rapid industrialization in 19th century Europe has caused this phenomenon as it was accompanied by rapid growth and concentration of working class people in overcrowded, poorly built houses (*Ibid.,* P. 77). In 1851, England passed the first legislation for building low income housing to certain minimum standards. And the laws for slum clearance was first enacted in 1868 (*Ibid.,* P. 77).

According to the studies on Bangalore slum, it is found that the slum-dwellers are overwhelmingly rural migrants (Godwin Shiri, *Our Slums: Mirror a Systemic Malady,*

Bangalore : ATC, 1999. P. 24). They are also employed as unskilled labourers (*Ibid.,* P. 25). Most of them also come from the dry areas (where there is only scanty and erratic rainfall and lack of river water) where poverty and illiteracy are rampant. The dalits and poor are also victims of caste- based oppressive feudal structure, so they migrate to promising nearby developing cities from the backward areas (*Ibid.,* p. 26). The industrialization and urbanization have also motivated the people to mobilize to the cities and caused to develop the slum.

The slums are located usually on low-living areas, by the side of railway tracks, on the sides of open drainage, at or on track beds, on the river banks, around or adjacent to apartments, below high tension wires, on hillocks, at the base of hillocks or in market places, observes Godwin Shiri (*Ibid.,* P. 34). According to Godwin Shiri "The unprecedented hike in land house value and rents in Bangalore from the 1980s has left its mark on the slums" (*Ibid.,* P. 36).

The condition of a slum

The living condition of the slum-dwellers is very pathetic. The slums are largely occupied by Hindu and Christian dalits. A big number of poor Muslims also occupy the slums. Slums is the reflection of the socio-economic inequalities. The poor are forced to live in unhealthy living conditions as they suffer from unemployment, poverty, illiteracy and powerlessness. The rich and powerful do push the poor to the periphery.

They have highly congested habitation and inadequate basic amenities (*Ibid.,* P. 31). The slum-dwellers suffer from lack of electric power, scarcity of water, depravity of the sanitary toiltes and bathrooms and there is no drainage system which cause serious health and hygienic problmes (*Ibid.,* PP. 54-57). In the rainy season the slum area is flooded with water and the people fall sick. Because of unhealthy conditions, they suffer from asthma, bronchitis, pneumonia, mental illness, rheumatism, ulcer, polio, tuberculosis and skin diseases (*Ibid.*, PP. 58-59).

Most of the slum-dwellers are unskilled and semi-skilled workers or involve in petty business. Some also are occupied in industrial sectors as skilled workers. Many involve in construction work, others work as Coolie, Watchmen, Cleaner, Gardners, Attender, Rag-pickers, Domestic servant, Loader, Driver, Printer, Electric worker, Plumber, Fitter and so forth (*Ibid.*, P. 62). Studies based on a slum-dwellers reveal that they involve in occupation such as Cobbler, Tailor, Cook, Broker, Mason, Petty shopowner, Vegetable seller and Flower-seller (*Ibid.*, P. 63).

The condition of the people reveals that the people in the slum are belonging to lower ladder of the society. They are migrating to cities for their survival. It is found that most of the slum-dwellers are migrated to Bangalore city because of economic deprivation. According to Godwin Shiri, the economic deprivation is the main reason for migration of dalit slum-dwellers in largest number as compared to other communities ["Urban slums : the tragedy of those who sought escape from rural caste class oppression - A case study" *Religion and Society* (March 1998) P. 17]. According to Shiri, "The slum-dwellers belong to the lowest economic strata as their occupation, income level and general living conditions amply reveal (*Ibid.*, P. 21).

A study on The thottumattam community (Kottayam, Kerala) also reveals the fact that the problem of this slum-dwellers are unemployment, poor housing and filthy environment (*Struggle Against Death*, Kottayam : educational Board for W. C. C. study programme, 1982. P. 99). They also lack convenience like latrine, water and electricity (*Ibid.*, P. 103). These are the common problems found in all the slums.

The common problem of the slums include poverty, Poor housing, inadequate water supply and electricity supply, inadequate sanitation (lack of toilet facilities), the water logging especially in the monsoon season result in water borne diseases like malaria, jaundice, cholera, viral fever and dysentry. The slum-dwellers are sometimes forcefully evacuated as part of slum clearance programme. They are also affected by inadequate drainage and as they live in cities they are victims of sound pollution along with water pollution. The people in the slum are also affected by Tuberculosis, Cancer, Hepatitis, Asthma and Chickenpox. Literacy rate among the slum children is also very low. The ill-treatment from school teachers and authorities and the economic crisis prevent them from education.

The Social situation

There are also social problems found in slum. The vices like drinking, drug, squandering, gambling, wife- beating, theft and prostitution are found in some slum (*Ibid.*, PP. 100-101). In the slum, there is no one to give moral and spiritual guidance to the members, so the moral laxity is found among them. Marriages are not mostly legally sanctioned. The marital life is like co-habitation.

Psychologically also the slum-dweller undergo severe stress as there is a crisis of identity, dignity and right. Their identity is not accepted by the society, and the Government does not accept their citizenship. They have no land of their own, and they may be evacuated at any time. The slum-dwellers are the alienated people as they are not regarded by the society.

A Response

Slum- dwellers are most alienated and marginated people

who need our care, love and support. It is important to rehabilitate them to provide proper basic amenities for a dignified living. This poorest of the poor in the society should be emancipated socially, economically, and spiritually. Their identity, dignity and right are to be upheld. Slum is the creation of the economic and social inequality which is to be tackled. In the power- encounter, the poor can find refuge only in the slums. They have the right to land, shelter, employment, citizenship, healthy environment and dignified survival.

The Government, voluntary organization, and the Churches can respond positively to the issues of the slum-dwelles. It is important to have solidarity with the struggles of the slum-dwellers. They are a suppressed humanity who are to be liberated from the clutches of the unjust structures. The rich need the services of the slum-dwellers, but do not like to accept their identity and their development. The structure is regulated by the dominant class, and is dehumanizing.

As God is identifying with the poor and powerless and liberating them, as Christians we are to participate in their struggle for dignity and rights (Lk 4:16-21). They have the right on land and have the right to food, education, employment and shelter. Policies are to made by the Government authorities to provide them adequate living condition. God's plan is a just and humane community (Lev. 25).

15

Response to HIV/AIDS, A Terrific Malady

The Human Immuno Deficiency Virus (HIV) or Acquired Immuno Deficiency Syndrome (AIDS) is spreading all over the world with a terrific pace. It is global epidemic. Each year 16,000 people are infected by AIDS. In 2001, around 33.6 million are AIDS affected. In India, there around 30.86 lakhs are infected by HIV. It is increasing in greater number in Maharashtra, Andhra Pradesh, Manipur and Tamilnadu. 60 per cent of sex workers in Bombay are affected by AIDS.

AIDS is mainly a Sexually Transmitted Disease (STD). It is transmitted by sex or through blood transfusion from the infected ones. The newborn babies are infected from the AIDS affected mother. The AIDS is spreading fast among intravenous drug users in Manipur and Nagaland. In India, it is found that 83 per cent of the AIDS infection is through sex contact. The illicit sex and the sexual relation with Commercial Sex Workers (CSW) has caused the AIDS.

The United Nations is working hard to prevent the spread of AIDS. It provided care and support for those infected and affected by the disease. The National Aids Control Programme (NACO) is directed to control the AIDS. They involve in the conscientization activities. Make aware the people the need for the use of condoms or contraceptives which can reduce the spread of AIDS. They also insisted the blood banks to strictly monitor the blood donors. They also involve in counselling.

AIDS is a serious epidemic which does not have any adequate medicine to cure. The only alternative is to prevent AIDS. For that a sane sex is very important. Sex should be limited to the marital partners, and when this rule is violated there is every possibility for men and women to become the carriers of AIDS. So much social stigma is attached to AIDS so the AIDS patients are always looked down upon by the society.

AIDS patients are also like any other patients who need our care and love. They are physically and psychologically affected. They are always under the stress and strain because of shame, ill health and also because of the fate. AIDS leads to sure death as there is no medicine to cure it. Though the AIDS patient is neglected, he or she has to be loved. The love to the sick shown by Jesus is a supreme example for the Church to follow with regard to the AIDS patients also. The Church can also involve in the conscientizing activities to reduce the spread of AIDS.

Africa is terribly affected by HIV/AIDS. Asia is also much affected by this deadly disease. In Africa almost a generation is wiped out because of HIV/AIDS. The babies are also victims of AIDS as their parents are HIV/AIDS patients. Not only the sex workers and homosexuals, anyone can be affected by HIV/AIDS as the illicient sex is increasing at an alarming ratio. Many newly wed are deceived by partners as they had been inflected by HIV/AIDS, so medical test before marriage is preferred. But this does not mean that partners are safe, as immoral practices can continue even after marriage. A sane sex order is possible only as fidelity to the partner is kept.

There is no clear evidence where HIV/AIDS is originated from. It was assumed that it was originated from African Monkeys. It is also observed that it must have originated from the homosexuality of American or Russian soldiers. It is also connected by some to the scientific research by which it is created and kept in the laboratory, from where this virus has escaped. All these theories are hypothetical. However, the gravity of its strike is disastrous.

According to Akhila Sivadas, "It is estimated that approximately 15 million children have been orphaned by HIV/AIDS Worldwide. Another startling figure is that everyday, about 1,800 new HIV infections in children under 15 are added to this figure, mostly by mother to children transmission". ("A roof of the orphaned" *The Hindu* (Sunday Magazine) November 30, 2008, P. 1)

The early detection of AIDS is crucial in treating it. The Anti Retroviral Therapy together with continuing nutritional and medical support can increase lifespan by twenty years or more, states Meenakshi Gautham ("Hope after HIV" (*The Hindu* (Sunday Magazine), 30th November, 2008. P. 1). One of the main things to monitor in HIV positive is monitoring the count of CD 4 cells. These cells are a variety of white blood cells that form the internal defense mechanism of the human body and they generate an antibody response to attacking organisms in the blood The virus attacks these cells and affecting the immune system (*Ibid.*, P. 1).

It is important to deal with 'people living with HIV and AIDS' (PLWHA) as 40 million HIV affected have no access to treatment. The virus that causes AIDS was first found in 1983 and this disease has become the fourth leading cause of mortality Worldwide. According to Nirmala Skill and Bennet Abraham, the HIV is a virus that attacks the immune system and it causes a steady decline in the T-4 cells which are the major components of the defense mechanism of our body, thus laying it open to deadly infections such as T. B, meningitis and various forms of pneumonia ("HIV/AIDS: medical scenario" *HIVAIDS : A Challenge to Theological Education,* edited by Samson Prabhakar and George Mathew Nalunnakkal, Bangalone: BTESSC/ SATHRI, 2009. P. 122).

There are several factors that leads to vulnerability to HIV/ AIDS. The poverty that induces the women to became commerical sex workers and they are yielding to this HIV/ AIDS. Many are ignorant of this deadly disease. Some people are infected as they do not keep sexual sanctity. Many women are victmized as their partners deceive them. So there is also gender issue in this case. Even children are victimized as they are not accepted by the society. There were cases where the HIV affected children were rejected by school authorities as the parents of other children in the school protested. Even the modern society is not having a proper awareness on the issue of HIV/AIDS. The innocent children are victimised as HIV/AIDS is transmitted from parents or as they are forced to sex (eg. child molestation and paedophilia), so it is an injustice to them.

The voluntary organization such as NGO's are working hard to conscientize the people. The Christian Churches are also aware of this problem, but not responding adequately to this problem. Our traditional understanding of Ministry is not conscious of these issues. As a preventive measure, the condoms are usually supplied by voluntary orgnizations and even Government agencies. But it is not the sole answer to the issue. The moral teaching is also a significant factor. The society also has to be conscientized so that the prejudice towards the victimized should go. Their care and rehabilitation are the Christian responsibilites. The human beings have the duty to care and support the diseased and marginalized ones. The HIV/ AIDS infected are psychologically, socially, physically, economically and spiritually affected, so a holistic perspective is needed to deal them.

God has created everyone in His image (Gen. 2:17). He also has a special concern towards the oppressed humanity (LK. 4: 16- 21). The HIV/AIDS patients are quite oppressed as the shame, neglect and rejection is attached to this epidemic. They are considered as the outcastes by the society, so it is important to restore their identity, dignity and rights as persons in the community. The HIV/AIDS infected are the new outcaste group as the lepers in the Jewish context. Jesus was ready to love, care and restore (healed them), them (Mt. 8:1-4; Mk 14 :3). Jesus had no aversion to the people who are infected by various diseases (Mt. 15: 29- 31). He touched them and healed them. God was willing to heal Naaman (2kgs. 5:1ff).

God has a preferential love towards those who are infected, afflicted and victimized. The Christian community is also called to serve the neglected and rejected ones. The HIV/AIDS infected are to be given counselling to raise their morals and hope. The ethical principles such as care, love and justice are to be applied dynamically for the welfare and liberation of the victimized. The measures are to be taken to curb the spread of the HIV/AIDS.

16

Christian view on Stewardship

God created the World and He made the human beings as the stewards of the whole creation. Steward is one who cares, oversees or manages things in a proper way. Stewardship is trusteeship. We are supposed to live responsibly considering others. Stewardship is not domineering or using undue authority. Stewardship challenges what is selfish and unjust. It upholds fairness and compassion.

The World is entrusted on human beings. We are to live together in love and harmony. The dictum of Lenin 'live and let live' is significant in this regard. John Ruskin's 'unto this last' and Gandhiji's 'sarvodaya'(Welfare of all) are based on the stewardship. It is very related to the idea, 'one for all, and all for one'. Gandhiji's concept of 'Antyodaya' (the rise of the least) is also very significant over here.

The hampering elements for the stewardship is selfish interests which is manifested in feudalistic/capitalistic spirit. Capitalism advocates the accumulation of wealth by any exploitative means. It regards the existence of few elites and never regard the existence of others, especially the marginated. The colonizers and the imperial spirits are not good stewards. They tap the resources for their own sake and leave the people into poverty. John Stuart Mill's idea ' maximum good to maximum number of people' could be a nearest ideal to stewardship. Stewardship has to transcend this idea and to be liberative.

A good steward manages his time properly. He will not spend time in vain. There are people who waste their valuable time by involving in gambling, which can even end up in rivalry and conflicts. The entertainments are also to be regulated, otherwise one can be an addict which can end up in misuse of time. The time management is very important in life. Gambling is waste of time and loss of money, and also it leads to unhealthy competition, gangwar and disharmony.

Even as we spend our wealth and money responsibly, we are not supposed to exploit others or use unjust means (e.g. bribes or getting money through unfair means) to gain wealth. We should have the willingness to share our resources for the good of others. Those who spend money for drinking, smoking and other ways are not good stewards. But it is important to share one's resources in order to serve the suffering humanity. It includes the sharing of resources for poverty alleviation, philanthropic work and development.

Stewardship is also concerned of the ecology. It is ecologically conscious. A good steward should have good foresight. It also looks forword. It is not only concerned of the present, but also of the future. It preserves the resources as it maintains the integrity of the whole creation. Stewardship protects the animal Kingdom and plant Kingdom. Good steward challenges the deforestation, injustices against the subaltern groups, selfish accumulation of resources, undue consumption of food and other resources and the pollution of soil, air and water.

An early reference to stewardship is found in Genesis1:28. There is indication about modern concept of authority here. It is not domination or rule which is meant in this context. The Hebrew word used here is'Rid' which refers the loving and caring relationship between the sheep and the shepherd. The real shepherd love, cares, and live for the sake of the sheep. Faithfulness is expected from the steward (Mt. 25: 14-23; 1Cor. 4:2).

Steward is understood as a person entrusted with management of another's property. He is a paid manager of a house or estate. Traditionally, Steward is associated to the feudal structure the rich being, lords or landlords. The attitude of a steward can king changes. He can be cruel, unfaithful or sympathetic. If he /she is sympathetic, they can be fair, and just in their dealing or responsibilities. A steward should be people-friendly and geneorus to take care of the welfare of everyone in equitable terms.

God is just in dealings. He liberates the people from the clutches of oppression and exploitation (Ex. 12) which is the ultimate aim of true stewardship. Stewardship is service as to take care of the responsibility (Act. 6). He should be even a responsible waiter at the table. He has to respond the needs (in the form of voices and cry) of the people.

Jesm was a faithful steward as he was exercising his responsibilites faithfully. He was creatively responding to the needs of the people. He fed the hungry (Mt. 15: 32-39), resolved the issue as they were in crisis (John. 2); he healed the sick as they cried out for help (John. 5). He was merciful to those who looked for help (Mt. 9:27-31). Jesus could find a good steward in the story of the good samaritan (Lk. 10: 5f).

17

The Issue of Suicide

There can be various reasons for suicide. It can be outcome of the deep depression. The reasons for suicide include (1) chronic illness, (2) psychological disorders, (3) failure in love-affairs, (4) failure in marital life, (5) financial crisis, (6) mental agony because of public shame, (7) failure in examinations, (8) depression out of unemployment, (9) harassment, (10) death of the beloved ones.

There are social, economic, psychological and genetic reasons behind the suicide. It is a last resort in the extremity of man. When a person feels that he/she cannot control the situation she/he opts for committing suicide. The modern man is psychologically upset as they are very anxious because of the unhealthy competition in the life situations. The psychological temper of human being is lost and trying to end life even for very simple reasons. Even a quarrel in a domestic situation sometimes leads to suicide. The Jihadis and guerilla groups commit suicide as human bombs on religious or ideological reasons.

There are different ways in which people commit suicide. Taking poison, hanging, drowning, jumping from top of the buildings, self- injury, getting electric shocks are some of the ways in which individuals choose to commit suicide. Groups or gangs do even force or inspire others to join the act of suicide. It is observed that children and the adults, the men and women, rich and poor, educated and uneducated, highly placed and lowly placed are all involved in committing suicide.

When a person is in utter despair and no hope, he or she prefers to commit suicide. It is nothing but a person is deciding to end ones own life by adopting his/her own means. It is chosen as a last resort by persons and groups to escape the crisis forever. They fail to realize any means to survive or withstand the crisis situation. The Latin word 'sui caedere' means kill oneself, so suicide means deliberately terminating one's life.

According to the National Crime Records Bureau, in 2005 the number of Indians comitted suicide is 1. 14 lakhs. It is also observerd of the 1.5 lakh Indian farmers who took their own lives between 1997 and 2005, nearly two-third did so in just the state of Maharashtra, Andhra Pradesh, Karnataka and Madhya Pradesh (including Chhattisgarh) (P. Sainath, "Farm suicide arising, most intense in 4 states" *The Hindu* (November 12, 2007) P. 11). 17,000 farmers committed suicide in 2005. In the state of Kerala also many farmers committed suicide. Prof. K. Nagaraj of the Madras Institue of Development studies observed that from the mid-90s onwards prices and farm income crashed, there is also cut in subsidies and cultivation costs shot up, which led to debt trap (*Ibid.,* P. 11). The crop failures, lack of irrigation facilities, lack of stability in the value of agricultureal products and the growing prices of fertilizes, pesticides and seeds affect the farmers badly.

Those who commits suicide should not be looked upon with contempt as they are victims of the situation. It is our responsibility to properly guide the persons to respect life. Recently in India, many farmers committed suicide because of the burden of agricultural loans. The agricultural products also do not get fair price which disappoints many farmers. No one is permitted to commit suicide. It is a crime done against the life of human beings.

The religious traditions are against the suicide as they consider it as sin. The Church authorities do not even bury them with full honours. But recently, some Churches come forward to realize the factors behind the suicide and willing to render a dignified burial. The traditional attitude towards those who commit suicide is radically changed.

It is important to avoid the tendency to commit suicide. The Church and society should work for creating a situation where a dignified life is possible. The life is to be nourished, and it should not be allowed to take it. Life is given by God and it is the precious gift of God. According to the Bible, those who commit suicide are accused. A value based orientation should be given to society by conscientization in order to give a proper perspective on human life. Respecting life is essential for the well-being of the humanity.

Suicide or taking one's life is considered as sin by the Bible. The sanctity of life is always promoted by Christianity. The Biblical command in decalogue 'Thou shall not kill' (Ex. 20 :13) and the concept 'do not harm ' in natural law have influenced St. Augustine and Thomas Aquinas to condemn suicide. Life is the gift of God and none has the right to terminate it. There are instances of King Saul (Isam. 31: 4-5), Ahitophel, Zimri (1kgs. 6: 18)and Judas Iscariot (Mt. 27:5) who committed suicide. Judaism, christianity, Islam, Hindusim, and Buddhism stand for sanctily of life. God is the source of life and Jesus Christ came to provide abundant life and life eternal (Jn. 3:16; 11:25; 10:10). Everyone is created in God's image(Gen. 1:27), so one's life has to be perserved and kept dignified. Life is the gift of God and no one has the right to destroy it.

18

Corruption, a Structural Evil

Corruption has become a way of life for our politicians and bureaucrats. Interestingly those who are supposed to upkeep the law and dispense justice involve in the different sorts of corruption. Instead of using their good offices for the interests of the people, they use their position and authority for their selfish motives.

The ideals, the morals and the rules are violated by the politicians and bureaucrats for bribes or "commission" (The term 'commission' stands for bribery which involves a large sum of money). The custodians of law such as the Judge and Magistrates have recently involved in the corruption as they manipulated their capacity for bribes. If the custodians of the law such as the police and the Judges are overturning justice, it is a severe problem.

The Bofors gun deal is now again comes to the scene. In the contract between Swedish firm and Indian Government, it is argued that certain politicians and middlemen have received around two hundred crore rupees as "commission". This money is given by the Swedish company only to sell their products. Usually the 'commission'(bribe) would be adjusted by the companies in the price of the product. Thus in the Bofors gun deal the bribe that is received by middlemen and politicians have gone from the pocket of the Indian Citizens.

In the Telecom scam, fodder scam of Bihar and in the coffin scam, it is reported that, crores of rupees received as bribe to the concerned persons. From top to bottom bureaucracy is corrupt. Indian politicians are after '*havala*' and 'commission' (Bribe). The higher officials and the attenders/peons are happy to receive bribe. In order to sanction a loan worth rupees 10, 000 one has to give one thousand as bribe and when the money is sanctioned another one thousand would be given. This is all done for the 'favours received' from the officials. The main question is why the people receive bribes.

(1) In the political sphere, it is a way of accumulating money for the next election. The politicians also see it as means to keep themselves wealthy. It will help them to have a luxurious life.

(2) The bureaucrats take bribe in order that they can have posh lifestyle. The money can be also used to send their children for Medicine or Engineering or other higher professional course. The bribe also can be a 'great help' for them to fulfil their aspiration to build huge house, and to buy land, Refrigerator, Television, Computer etc. The politicians and bureaucrats found it as a short cut to become rich within a short period of time.

(3) The low grade employee either receives directly or joins with the officers to get bribe is to fill their need gap.

The corruption is outcome of selfish interests. In order to achieve the goals, people use or tempt to use false or unjust means. The false motives includes obtaining academic degree and employment through crooked means and overturning justice by bribing the police officers, judicial officers and civil authorities. The corruption includes the bribing higher officials to obtain promotions.

It is a known fact that the Indian bureaucracy is corrupt. Though there are rare exceptions, almost all officers are corrupt. Only those who have money power could get prompt services from the Government offices. The condition of the poor is so pathetic. Their rights are always overturned. Money is a means to manipulate the officials and also it is a means to enjoy the 'good' services of the offices.

Corruption has become a culture in the Indian society. Corruption is also a Worldwide phenomenon. Since corruption become a way of life, it has developed itself as a culture. Top to bottom, the Indian society needs a purgation. Only when the politicians and the bureaucrats have a sense of justice the corrupt structure can be reformed. It is also important to have a united effort of the people to check the corruption by challenging the centres of corruption. Corruption is found in many development projects in India which is assisted by World Bank. Recently the World Bank has found cases of fraud and corruption in development projects in India receiving bank aid relating to malaria control, health system development, food and drug capacity building, national HIV/AIDS control and tuberculosis control (Ramesh Thakur, "Fighting the Cancer of Corruption" *The Hindu* (January 25, 2008), P. 10).

Ramesh Thakur observes, "corruption robs civic life of public virtue. The World Bank estimates that corruption amounts to 5 per cent of the World economy, well over $ 1. 5 trillion. The effects of corruption are most destructive and savage in developing countries. Not coincidentally, the top 20 countries the 20 least corrupt-in Transparency Imternational's annual survey tend to be dominated by the Western industrialized countries especially the northern Europeans, Canada and New Zealand" (*Ibid.,* P. 10).

The Bureaucrats, the politicians, the police and judiciary are found corrupt. Corruption is an Asian tragedy. It is reported that the main issue in Asian countries is corruption involving politicians, civil servants and law enforcement officers (*Ibid.,* P. 10).

Corruption is a human violation on the citizen's rights, especially the rights of the powerless are denied. They can obtain even the right or what is deserved only by giving bribes. The corruption is acute in India, especially the states of Bihar. China, India and Indonesia are found as the worst corrupt countries. Among the Asian countries, Japan and Singapore rank among the least corrupt. Most of the corrupt leaders are belonging to Asia, Africa and Latin America.

An amount is kept by compnies for every deal to give as bribes, which will make the deal fictitious. The middle-men used to get this amount. This bribe in the form of 'commission' is enticing the parties to their deal. In all deals including the arms deal, the cancer of corruption is found.

It is important to curb the illicit gains of few people in the form of bribery. It is a challenge to stewardship, democracy, human rights and justice. On October 31, 2003, the UN General Assembly adopted historic treaty (UN Convention against corruption) against global corruption in order to grapple with the issue of bribery and embezzlement.

The privileges and benefits that are meant for the poor are even snatched away by the bureaucrats. The officers and politicians are to be bribed to get privileges. The rights and privileges are not given unless the officeres are bribed. This is the condition in Indian context. In the context of reconstruction of Afghanistan also it is observed that corruption in the form of bribery is found. Clancy Chassay has reported that in order to get contract from a foreign firm, a contractor has to pay a ten per cent bribe and that become culture or way of life ("corruption blights reconstruction" *The Hindu* (February 20, 2009). P. 13). It is observed that there is corruption, but there is no way of documenting it, as there is no proper records of how much money is spent, and where it comes from (*Ibid.*, P. 13).

Corruption is inhuman and it is crime against humanity, especially to the poor. It is an illicit means by which things are done and bribery is payment given or asked which is not deserved for getting things done. The bribery is also given for getting things done or getting position unjustly. According to Lord Acton power corrupts, and absolute power corrupt absolutely.

Corruption as an inhuman and unjust practice is condemned by the Bible. The injustices are not tolerated by God. The greed for money (1Tim. 6:10; Eph. 5:3; Mt. 6:24), obtaining material or money by unjust means (Prov. 15:27; 17:23; Jere. 17:11), and overturning justice (Jere. 5:28; Am. 5:10-12) are hated by God. John the Baptist also stood vehemently against corruption(Lk. 3:13, 14). Jesus preached on repentance and Kingdom of God which were a challenge to structural evil and corruption. Zachaeus was even willing to return the money that he received unjustly. He was conscious of the corrupt practice.

Corruption is a crime against God and man. It is a structural evil. It breeds wickedness and injustices. It is an oppressive practice, especially against poor and powerless. The Christian Community and the civil society have to conscientize the people to protest the corrupt structures. A prophetic mission is to be upheld in order to deal with corruption.

19

An Analysis and Appraisal of the Development Concepts

Introduction

The history of development began after the Second World War. The discovery of hunger and poverty and under - development attracted the attention of many. The United Nations took initiative to control the situation. The General Assembly of the United Nations on the proposal of John Kennedy declared 1960's as "the Development Decade".

So many models can be found for the question of development. The Government, the international agencies and the social organisations are involved in this attempt to development. Since the models or approaches are found unsatisfactory, the debate is going on. This is an attempt to describe what has been the major understanding and the strategic responses. How are these to be evaluated is also a concern of this attempt

The Concept of Development

The concept 'development' was emerged after the Second World War. In the context of post World War as there was shortage of food. The hunger and poverty were prevailed. The prospective such as 'developed', 'developing' and 'under developed' are also Involved and 1960's and 1980's are also declared by UN as development decades. The word 'development' is closely related to social, economic and religious development. It is meant for the development of infrastructures – the roads, health system, educational system, telecommunication , electricity, water supply and housing. Development indicates progress in all areas of life, which includes science and technology, agriculture and industry. There is rural and urban development. There are also concept like community development and rehabilitation. The right to food, right to shelter, right to education, right to health, right to clothing and right to employment are inevitable factors in development. Development should be holistic and holistic development also include the empowerment of poor ; dalits, tribals, victimized women, fisherfolk, slum-dwellers and other marginalized groups.

The eco-justice, social and economic justice, gender justice and political justice are also playing vital role in the concept of development. The development is related to transformation. The holistic transformation is significant in relation to development. Mission should aim at the development of the people as it is people's development. Justice, freedom, equality and self-reliance are integral to the concept of development. The development has to be people-friendly as it should not violate the rights of the people. Certain form of 'development' are meant for the benefit of the capitalists. The best examples for violation of right to land is found in Narmada Valley, Nandigram and Singur, where people are forcefully evaluated for the sake of " development".

1. The Main Approaches of Development: Analysis and Reponses

The debate on development is going on in the secular and Christian realm. The following are some of the main approaches traced by Richard Dickenson.

(a) The Capitalist Approach

According to Dickenson "This view proposes to generate development primarily through " free market" forces of supply and demand" *(To set at liberty, the oppressed,* Geneva:WCC, 1945. p. 62). He states again that the Government allows the free forces to have their function in the sphere of business. In the capitalist model, there is private ownership and free international trade. The private ownership of means of production is another feature. The firms decide the what and the how of production and the management will control the whole system. In the capitalist economy, the workers do not have any right on farm or land. They 'sell their labour to the capitalist firm in order to obtain a wage with which to buy necessities of the life' (*Ibid.,* p. 62).

The defenders of this approach argue that this model will provide industrialization and employment. It generates, in their view, technical and managerial skills. They will also argue that 'it links poorer countries with a network of resources, financing and marketing' (*Ibid.*, p. 62). On the other hand, the opponents of this approach say that it will end up in the monopoly of political and economic power. It will, in their opinion, create irrational priorities, exploitation of natural resources, exploitation of the poor and social injustice. Another valid argument is that " technology of transnational corporations is capital intensive than labour intensive" (*Ibid.,* p. 62).

(b) United Nations Approach

In the words of Dickenson, it recognizes the National

Government as the foremost agents of change. The basic assumptions such as economic growth, capitalization, technological applications and industrialization are related to the capitalist model. The infrastructure such as roads, health, communication and education are the main problems of developing countries. So the U. N. provides help through their different wings for the development.

Those who are against this model would say that U.N. is very optimistic of the Government leaders. It is bureaucratic. It pays little attention to the change of people. It is a "top-down" approach. It emphasizes the technological development. Some feel that the U.N. model has its support from industrialized societies (*lbid.* , p. 65).

(c) Change-political-Structure Approach

This approach links with socialist ideology. It looks for a new political order since the present political system is found as a failure and present Government as a systemic violence. This approach is for total change. It is revolutionary. It is closely linked to Martian view. The opponents hold the view that the new system or order also may not be non-oppressive. They further argue that the change of structure and values and thoughts are essential to have a real change (*lbid.*, P. 65)

(d) Conscientization Approach

This model stresses people's participation at the local level. Paulo Friere is a strong supporter of this model. According to this approach, development should be initiated by oppressed and poor. It gives less importance to the development initiated by leadership. The action should be controlled by the powerless. For the success of this model, they should be conscientized. Conscientization is to awaken the people's consciousness, their capacities and rights.

The people become more important than the structure in this approach. Those who oppose this model have the opinion that it does not address the systemic power. They also believe that it is too pessimistic of the radically reformed and new political structure to organize people's participations (*Ibid.* , pp. 66ff).

(e) Radical Political Economy Paradigm

This is a socialistic pattern. According to James Weaver and Kenneth Jameson, the following are the characteristics of this model: This approach would agree that people are rational and people act together to produce surplus. The good life includes the ability to meet basic needs and it involves social activities. According to this approach, good society has to ensure consumer sovereignty. The worker's sovereignty must be facilitated. Good society is one which provides a mechanism to aggregate people's preference for community and good society must acceptably solve the problem in equality. This is a Marxian approach.

The political economists evaluate the economic system with the following criterion (1) that which provides for everyone's basic needs, (2) that which provides everyone with meaningful work, (3) satisfying human relationship, (4) healthy environment, (5) society based on equality (*Economic Development:competing paradigms*, London: University Press of America, 1981. p. 55).

(f) Growth with Equity Approach

There was an understanding that the growth of production and GNP will enable the poor to come up. But it was found out later that it was a misconception. Without equal distribution, growth will not help. The following growth with equity variants are the suggestions of some experts.

This is found in the book' *Economic Development: competing paradigms*'by Kenneth Jameson and James Weaver:

1. *The employment generation:*ILO found that small-scale industries are profitable and employment generating.
2. *Redirecting investment* :Chenery argues that the poor must have the income which can meet their needs (*lbid.,* p. 53). The suggestion is that if investment can be directed towards projects that are labour-intensive and which also meet basic needs, there will be improvement in the lot of poor majority.
3. *Meeting basic needs :* This approach was put forward by Mahbubul-Haq of World Bank. It gives importance to food, shelter, literacy, medicine, sanitation, and nutrition.
4. *Human resource development :* Irma Adelman argues for redistribution of productive assets, that "provision must also be made to ensure continued access to assets and necessary agricultural inputs for the poor, once the distribution has taken place" (*lbid.* , p. 10).
5. *Agricultural and rural development* :It creates employment and supplies enough food. The rural small-scale industry, minor-developments and projects are important.
6. *New international economic order :* Existing order is favouring inequalities. So a new order is essential. NIEO is based on basic needs approach. "NIEO stresses the need for structural changes in world economic and trading relationships to diminish national dependency. The basic goal of NIEO is to move from

> dependent to interdependent economic and political structure. Among major goals of the NIEO are increased aid, new and stable commodity agreements. . . "(*Ibid.* , p. 54ff).

(g) Summary of some other perspectives

Under this heading some of the popular approaches are to be discussed. The first two are welfare approach and modernization approach. The welfare approach is the work spontaneously done by the humanists and social reformers. The modernization approach is more equal to the westernization and industrialization.

There are two other perspectives such as growth paradigm and dependency view. The growth paradigm "assumes that standard of living, definable in composite ways though GNP or per capita consumption of essential commodities, is the goal of development"(Dickenson, *op. cit* p. 26). The dependency view "stresses the tension and disharmony of interests between the centres of economic and political power and the "periphery" of marginalized persons and nations who are usually in the majority. Rather than a partnership of interests, the powerful exert and extend their power though the further subjugation and dependency of the " powerless" (*Ibid.*, p. 27). C. Elliot has found development as humanization and liberation, since it is an attempt to liberate and to make people more human. C. T. Kurian has rightly said "...... development becomes liberation and the narrow or limited concern for development will have to enlarge take into account liberation in the economic sense, in the social sense, in the cultural and political sense, in the spiritual sense" [C. T. Kurien, "widening perspective on Development ". *Bangalore Theological* forum vol. XIX, No. 3, (1987), p. 137].

II. Development Strategic Responses

In the patterns of development there are some new orientations and strategic ideas evoloved (Dickenson, *op. cit*, p. 80). These are the new attempts. The experts evaluated the development programmes and tried to make some responses on the basis of it.

(a) New Orientations

1. *Liberation :* The concept of development and liberation are found fluid. The Montreux 1 Conference in 1970 suggested the self-reliance, economic growth and social justice which has psychological, political, social and economic dimensions.
2. *Disenchantment with Western models :* The Western models are industrial, so there is erosion of humanitarian values — cultural disintegration and personal alienation. Parmar has opinėd that the Gandhian model is appropriate for Indian context.
3. *Significance of structural change :* It is crucial but the elements of vested interests like to maintain *status quo.*
4. *Change groups :* A pessimism has developed on the ability of the National Government and the international agencies. It is argued that basic changes can be brought by the local change groups, since the social structure, ideas, and values can be oppressive. Friere suggests to overcome "values" by literacy and *local conscientization.*
5. *Enrichment and improvement :*There was a misunderstanding that the creation of more

wealth is the answer to poverty. But this was replaced by the importance of cultivation of human skills and general education.

6. *Cultural fissures :* The ethnic, religious, linguistic, class and caste difference are found to be the impediments of social and economic development. This view has changed very drastically. Today, culture context is important even for doing theology.
7. *Development of education* :It promotes to make the rich realize that they are propagating poverty. It is to raise consciousness for global justice.

(b) Strategic ideas

1. The poorest of the poor are becoming the main concern. In India 40 per cent of the people are below the poverty line. In China, the attention to this has enabled progress. Rural community development is emphasized.
2. Attempts were made to elevate the status of women. This was a move to protect their rights.
3. There is a changing view on projects. The Church-sponsored projects are found producing not much goodness. The local level decision is given more preference. Efforts are made to indigenize development decisions for projects. The mobilization of local resources is asked for (moratorium on aid). There is also a change from mini-projects to comprehensive programmes.
4. Rural sector is given prominence: Rural community development with stress on consciousness and participation.

5. Concern is made to take care of unempolyment. The need for the change of educational system is hailed to resolve the problem. The unemployed and underemployed are given much priority.

III. Development Paradigms : Latin American, Socialist and Asian Cases

Its good to look at the following cases to see how their programmes had worked in this context. Some of the cases had very positive effects.

(1) Two orthodox cases : Latin American

(a) Brazil

The following are the characteristics of Brazil's development in the words of Kenneth Weaver and Jameson:

1. Government intervenes with price, tax and wage in order to keep market operating effectively.
2. Government enterprises are substantial in electricity, banking, steel and petroleum.
3. Government affects income distribution by the tax structure and enforcement of its wage policy.
4. The foreign investment is encouraged but regulated.
5. Brazil tried to become export-oriented.
6. Reliance of collaboration with private enterprise and the development of a free enterprise system, e.g. there were efforts to develop a stock market and to mobilize domestic carvings.

(b) Chile

The following factors are the features of Chilean model.

1. Cut the role of the Government in economy.
2. The Government enterprises are sold to private entities.
3. Opening up to the international market.
4. Government control of price.
5. Income-tax is cut drastically.
6. Money supply growth must be shown and strictly controlled so as to wring out the economy, the inflation which exists there. There were advantages and failures in this orthodoxy. The GNP has increased to an average of 7 per cent during 1976-77. The fishing, construction industries were growing. But the growth of employment was sluggish. There is a decline in availability of goods. The consumption had declined among the poorest. This orthodoxy was found inadequate in the areas of unemployment, income inequality and absolute poverty.

2. The socialist cases

The Socialist countries like Russia, Cuba and China achieved the power by revolution. The ownership in these countries is by Government. This is pre-condition for any socialism. The state has more power and decisions are made by state. The presupposition of the Russian policy was that the " rapid industrialization, centrally planned within a system of state ownership of the means of production, would provide the basis for massive increase in consumption in the future "(James Weaver and Kenneth

Jameson, *op cit*; p. 115). But Chinese strategy concentrates on agriculture. They promote a collective agriculture. "The peasants are encouraged to have co-operative form of farming"(*Ibid.* , p. 118). The Soviet Russia broke up because of bureaucratic corruption and ill-planning. China and Cuba still exist as they progress with their strategies.

3. Asian cases

(a) Taiwan Model

The agriculture is central to them. Agriculture is playing a key role in financing industrialization too. The rural industrialization is given importance. In fact, the rural industrial employment rose from 47 per cent to 52 per cent between 1956 and 1966. The technology in both industry and agriculture were carefully guided to use labour (*Ibid.* , p. 78).

Because of the careful use of technology and the attempt to develop the rural areas, the development in Taiwan is taking a good shape.

(b) Indian Model

The Government of India has done so many things on development programmes. The five year plans are one among the programmes. The Rural development is also one of the concerns of Indian Government. Emphasis is also given to areas of health, rural industries and education. The Gandhian model pays"attention to the key role of villages in the advancement of society"(Somen Das. "Theological-Ethical critique of Modern Development" *BTF* vol. XIX, No. 3 (1987), (P. 201). But this model is neglected and India is after Western models. The community development programme started in 1951. It emphasizes that "all sectors of village activity are considered as an organic whole covering agriculture, poultry, farming, education, health and sanitation"(K.Mathew Kurien, "Critique of Rural Development Programme" *BTF* vol. XIX, No. 3 (1987) p. 144). The Integrated Rural Development programme was meant for the poorest of the poor. India follows a mixed economy. Capitalist model and socialist models play their role in Indian situation. The pathetic fact is that the beneficiaries of these programmes are not the poor , but rather the rich and middle class. That's why 40 per cent of the people are still below the poverty line. The land is in the hands of the rich so the agriculture programmes are not aiming at the landless poor and the labours. The illiterate poor of India are not aware of many programmes. The poor are powerless so they are cheated and exploited by others. So unemployment and inequality are not tackled properly in the Indian situation. The undue importance given to modernization has been found as an important problem for this condition. A structural change is essential in Indian situation. The fascination for liberalization policy is also affecting the poor badly. The inclination to capitalism is to be curbed. The United progressive alliance (Congress-led alliance) ensures the employment (National Rural Employment Guarantee Act) and shelter and economic assistance to women, widows and the old. Rural housing was given through Indira Awaas Yojana.

IV. The Evaluation

Self-reliance is an emerging concern in the realm of Development. The Gandhian model is oriented to this, according to Parmar. Dag Hammarskjold project of development and International co-oporation 1975 had found the following characteristics for an 'alternative development' paradigm. According to it the emphasis should be : (1) need oriented, (2) endogamous-stemming from the heart of each society, (3) self- reliant- relying in its own strength and resources, (4) ecologically sound - utilizing natural resources considering the ecological system, (5) based on structural transformation the aim should be to change the structure which is economic and social (Quoted from Richard Dickenson's *Poor, yet making many rich* p. 32ff).

The findings are useful for any programme or model of development. But this is not enough. The ultimate goal of development has to be the equality of all. It should not stop with need-oriented or basic need approach. The aspect of self-reliance is good, but it can be possible only through a radical restructuring of the society. The fair distribution of resources should be stressed. The approaches of models discussed in this chapter have their merits and demerits. The main concern of any Development Model should be to eradicate poverty. It should provide employment to all, and enhance equal distribution of assets and production and even equal access to the facilities such as sanitation, health, transportation and education. The per capita income should be increased and it should gradually lead to equality. The Development Model is a failure if that is not meeting the needs of the poorest of the poor.

All models can be evaluated with some criterion : whether it makes sure the fair distribution of all facilities to all people. The land reforms and distribution is also another important aspect. But these are not exclusive criterion. If the gulf between the rich and poor are not narrowing down, the development models are a failure. The Development Models should be designed in order that it may cater to the solutions to the problems of people from the lowest strata of the society. All countries should develop their own indigenous model of development rather than following western model. Then only it will suit the context of a particular country. It is neither United Nations model nor capitalist model nor liberation model which is important, but the model which should evolve from the context. This model also consider the participation of all, especially the powerless poor. If their voice is unheard in the planning process, what is the need of development ? If we ask the question, for whom the development, the answer must be, for the poor. The Development also has to emphasize the change of structure. The relative improvement will not do much help. Mathew Kurian observes that, in India, the Western model (capital intensive) was used so the rural agricultural sector was excluded for a long time. Because of this, we have not yet achieved the eradication of unemployment, poverty and socio-economic inequalities and the promotion of self-reliant development and establishment of socialistic patterns of society (K. Mathew Kurian, *op. cit*, p. 145). The Western approaches caused ecological problems in Indian context. The multinational corporations established by Western collaboration was to tap the resources and raw materials. These models will help only the rich and the capitalists.

A more sustainable development is essential. According to Volker Heins, sustainable society is possible by making economic growth more equitable and eco-friendly ["the importance of being earthly" Religion and Society Vol. 43, No. 4 (Dec. 1996), P. 5]. Sustainable development is concerned of bio-diversity, farm land and water resources. It questions the over exploitation and polluting the environment (*Ibid.* , PP. 5-7).

The conscientization should be done on the rich, since the rich are irresponsible to the society, especially to the poor by keeping and using wealth very selfishly. We must look forward to a model which can provide opportunities and power equally to all. It should not accommodate feudalism. The decision-making power will go into the hands of the rich, if they hold the income-generation resources. So the first step towards constructive development can be the land reform and fair distribution of land to all. This was an admirable factor which had taken place, mainly, in the socialist countries. Here the role of the change of socio-economic structure should be noticed. Each country has to learn their socio- economic and political situation and develop an approach in accordance with their observation. In Latin American and Asian contexts, the rich are powerful and the poperty is in their hands. So the condition of the poor cannot be improved, unless this situation is changed. The economic development should be based on a structural change in the economic system.

The model of development we foresee should shake the structures and elements of *status quo*. This development approach also has to have the maximum participation of all people regardless of gender differences. It should be sustainable and people oriented. The women and the youth must get participation. All development projects should involve the people from the local area in order that they can be the instruments of change. The approaches such as change—political structure, approach and conscientization approach have very crucial roles to play in order to bring radical changes in the society, so that the poverty may be alleviated. After a thorough review of the development programmes and models the scholars have come to some strategic responses *i.e.*, the new orientations and strategic ideas. The issue of development is not really an easy one. So debate on this issue is continued.

Conclusion

All through the history of 'development' various models have been introduced. These approaches served the purpose to an extent. Once the Western models were found fascinating, but today these models are critically analysed. The inference is that the developing countries should go for their own models. The dependence on Western models is not an answer, since the poverty remains same in almost all the developing countries. We have been following a 'top-down' model, but the time has come to think of an approach which is 'bottom-up'. We should have a people-oriented liberative model. An adequate development model should be ecologically conscious and it has to aim at the welfare of all, especially the marginated (Dalits, tribals and women).

20

Ragging, Party Politics and the Inhumanity

Ragging and party politics are making unrest in the student world. The brutal nature of man emerges in certain situations and so much of harm is done by it. The harassment, threatening and the psychological and physical torture in the name of ragging and party politics disclose the fact that the forces of evil are very much prevalent in the society.

Ragging

Ragging has become a common phenomenon in schools and colleges, especially in the professional colleges (*e.g.* Engineering Colleges and Medical Colleges). Ragging is the reflection of the saddist mind. Man has the trait to manipulate and dominate others which comes out in the form of harassment and torture. This anti-social element is a blot on civilized society. The senior students demand money from juniors, forcing to copy classnotes for them, stripping the clothes of juniors and even beat them.

These are instances by which the freshers are continuously harassed or tortured so they dropped the studies. The acute forms of ragging that leads even to the death of new students. There are also cases of students committing suicide as they are hurt psychologically and physically. If the freshers are complaining to the authorities about the torture, they are further harassed and beaten up inside and outside the campus. This situation has created an unrest and disturbance to parents also as they feel that their children are insecure.

According to the Concise Oxford Dictionary, ragging means scolding, teasing, tormenting, disorderly conduct or rowdy celebration. It is an unhealthy and rough dealing of seniors and the dominant groups over the juniors and the powerless to affirm their leadership, dominance and authority. This kind of harassment and torture are done also over the women, dalits, tribals, blacks and other powerless ones by dominant class. The upper castes force even the dalit women to walk naked through the streets.

Ragging is a crime against humanity. This inhumanity does the psychological and physiological torture and even preventing the people from contiuning their studies. The anti-ragging cell is helping the students who are undergoing the trouble, but those who complains are even futher ragged by other students as the protection is insufficient from Government authorities (e.g. police) and the college or school authorities. The society, the Government, the college authorities and the parents have to play a responsible role in order to stop this oppressive element. The most effective step can be taken by institutions and the parents who can have a constant vigil of the situation.

Party-Politics

The ideological conflict between the political parties lead to unhealthy competition and confrontation. There is threatening and physical assault in the name of party - politics. This conflicting situation is found in the schools, colleges and in the society as a whole. There are cases also of throwing stones at each other, stabbing and killing for the sake of the party. The conflict between students of different political parties are disturbing the studies and it creates an insecure and theatening situation in schools and colleges. The conflicts are common in the society also in the name of politics. Ther are gang wars and killing for the interests of the political parties. This becomes acute in schools, colleges and in the society at the time of elections to administrative bodies.

There is a criminality in politics or criminalization of politics which is a dangerous situation. There is also politicizing of religion by which the hindutva forces challenge the secularist values and the minority rights. They attacked the minority communities in Ayodhya, Godhra, Orissa (Kandhamal) and in several other places. Pseudosecular forces are using religion for the political interests. This brings disharmony, hatred, distrust, killings and mass massacre.

The community has to have peace and justice which are integral to the Kingdom of God. The harmonious existence among students and others are essential for the stability and integrity of a nation. We are to undergird each other and not to undermine. Disturbing the life of other is a crime and inhumanity. A community can exist only if there is love, unity, support and care. Mutuality is a key factor in human relationship, so also the humanness. 'Love our neighbour as yourself' (Luke 10: 25ff) is the teaching of Jesus which is central to the formation of a just and humane community.

21

Human Right Violations on the Minorities of India

The human rights is an important issue in the context of dehumanization. The rights of the people are denied everywhere, and especially the minorities are undergoing severe threat from the fascist forces. Their right as a citizen is not protected by the Government as the religious fundamentaiists challenge their right to existence.

Human Rights : A Perspective

It is the right of every person to live in dignity. According to Felix Wilfred "human rights is a question of regulating right relationships in society among individuals or groups-relationship which are humanizing and therefore fair and just" (Lobo George V. *Human Rights in Indian situation,* New Delhi:CBCI, 1991. p. VI)

Human right is part and parcel of Social Justice. In the context of colonization, poverty, domination and exploitation, there is no dignity to anyone as the rights are denied. The poor and powerless or victimized are living in unjust and dehumanizing situation, so their right and dignity are to be restored for their liberation. There is no justice without rights. The human rights is offered by the Constitution of India and UN declaration of human rights. It is not a mercy or charity. The freedom and justice are playing significant roles in human rights.

There are wrong notions about human rights. It is not *charity,* It is not *development,* It is not *compassion.* It is based on equal status. It is equal opportunities in employment, education, and professing religion. It is the right to live without discrimination. Sophists (5th century BC) hold that 'Just or right means nothing but what is the interest of the stronger party'. For Aristotle, the women, children and slaves are inferior in status. For Romans also slaves and women were inferior in dignity and status. According to Russeau, man is born free, but everywhere he is in chains. The French Revolution affirms, 'Liberty, Fraternity and Equality'.

According to French declaration of rights (1789, 1790, 1791) :

(1) Men are born and remain free and equal in rights.

(X) No one should be harassed for his opinions, even religious opinions, provided that they do not disturb public order as established by law.

(XI) Freedom of thought and expression is one of the most precious rights of man.

In the UN declaration of human rights, it is stated.

(1) All human beings are born free and equal in dignity and status.

(2) Everyone is entitled to all the rights and freedoms set forth in this declaration without distinction of any kind, such as race, colour, language, or religion

(3) Everyone has the right to life, liberty and security of person.

(4) Everyone has the right to freedom of thought, conscience and religion, this right includes freedom to change his religion or belief and

freedom, either alone or in community with others and in public or private, to manifest his religion or belief in teaching, practice, worship and observance.

Indian Constitution

Art-14. "The state shall not deny to any person equality before the law or the equal protection of laws within the territory of India".

Art -15 (1) "The state shall not discriminate against any citizen on grounds of religion, race, caste, sex, place of brith or any of them".

Art-25 (1) Subject to public order, morality and health— all persons are equally entitled to freedom of conscience and the right freely to profess, practice and propagate religion".

Art-26 Subject to public order, morality and health, every denomination or any section thereof shall have the right :-

(a) To establish and maintain institution for religious and charitable purposes
(b) To manage its own affairs in matters of religion
(c) To own and acquire movable and inmovable property
(d) To administer such property in accordance with the law.

The minorities and their rights

The minorities are considered as the group of people who holds the religion or language which is not professed or spoken by the majority. Here we concentrate more on the religious minorities who are persecuted by the dominant religious groups. It should be kept in mind that there are linguistic and religious minorities. The minorities of India include Christians and Muslims.

According to 1981 Census, Hindus constitute 82.64 per cent, Muslims 11.35 per cent, and Christians 2.43 per cent. Louis Wirth, an eminent sociologist defines minority as follows:

> "We may define a minority as a group of people who because of their physical or cultural characteristics, are singled out from the others in the society in which they live for differential and unequal treatment and who therefore regard themselves as objects of collective discrimination. The existence of a minority in a society implies the existence of a corresponding dominant group with higher social status and greater privileges. Minority status carries with it the exclusion from full participation in the life of the society ("The problem of minority groups" Ralph Linton(ed). *The Science of Man in the World Crisis 1945.*)

The minorities have the cultural and educational rights:

Art. 29 (2). No citizen shall be denied admission into any educational institution maintained by the state of receiving aid out of state funds on grounds only of religion, race, caste, language, or any of them.

Art. 30 (1) All minorities, whether based on religion and language shall have the right to establish and administer educational institution of their choice.

(2) The state in granting aid to educational institutions shall not discriminate against minority institutions.

The dalit Christians are denied of their rights on the basis of religion, as Articles 14 & 15 of the Indian Constitution do not accept any kinds of discrimination on the grounds of religion, race, caste or place of birth. Art. 341, which empowered the President to form a list of scheduled castes explained that only Hindus are scheduled castes and no other. In 1960, the Sikhs, Jainists and Buddhists are recognized as Hindus and listed among dalits, and Christians are not included.

Articles 14-18 of the Indian Constitution affirm the equality of all citizens, regardless of religion. Articles 25-28 provide the right of the freedom of conscience, the right to profess, practice and propagate religion.

The Minorities Commission was established by the Central Government by a resolution dated 12th January, 1978 to safeguard the interests of the minorities.

The Anti-conversion bills are passed by Himachal Pradesh (1978), Arunachal Pradesh (1978), Madhya Pradesh (1968) and Orissa, (1978) Gujarat (2003), Rajasthan (2006), Chhattisgarh (2006), Tamilnadu (2004, later it was revoked), which restricts the Conversions to Christianity. Not only that Christians are persecuted without any reasons being a Christian is a crime for them. Their dignity and rights are challenged. Forcible re-conversions are done by Hindu fundamentalists in the name of '*shuddhi*'.

They attack the following:

(a) The structures of worship (Mosque/Church)

(b) The institutions (Educational, Medical)

(c) The leaders of the minority religions.

(d) The members of the minority religions.

Hindutva ideology is a threat to human rights. It is fundamentalistic and fascist. It is non-secularistic and non-human. They attacked minorities in different ways. Babri Masjid was demolished in December 6, 1992. They also have claim over 3000 mosques. They have killed Graham Staines and two sons on January 22, 1999.

Godhra Carnage, (Gujarat) was in 2002. Kandhamal (Orissa) Carnage (2008) was by Hindu fundamentalists against Christians. More than 60 people were killed and around 200 Churches were destroyed and thousands of Christians find refuge in forests and refugee camps.

If political freedom is our birth right (as Balagangadhar Tilak talked about political freedom), the religious freedom is also our birth right. Every one has the right to choose their political/religious ideology. Being a Christian does not loose their Constitutional rights, as an Indian. The fear of the dominant religious groups which resulted in the threat/Persecution over the individual/groups to move towards their religion of choice. There is right for every individual to move from one religion to another, which should be honoured. Constitutionally fraudulent means and use of force only are prohibited in the issue of conversion.

The Christian Responsibility

1. Be aware of the human rights. We should know our Constitutional rights.
2. There should be an organized effort to move the authorities against the human right violations.
3. Create an awareness among other dominant groups about the Constitutional rights/human rights.
4. The voice of protest should be made known in the state level, national level, and international level bodies or forums of human rights.

Bible affirms always the rights of the marginated and oppressed. Rights of Refugees (Dt 19:1-13), rights on prisoners of war (Dt 20:14) rights of fugitive slaves (Dt 23:15-16) right to marginated (gleaning rights) (Dt 24: 19-21), and fair wages to fugitives (Dt 24: 14-15) are upheld by the Bible. The minorities and their rights are protected by the Bible. Bible states that the fugitives (the minorities) should not be oppressed, as the Israelites were also fugitives in Egypt (Ex. 22:21).

Conclusion

There are various issues that are found in our context. These issues are creating a threatening situation as they are very inhuman. The dehumanizing forces are at work in every sphere which are to be tackled, otherwise our life is going to be very miserable. We are born with freedom and rights to live in a dignified way on this planet. So it is important to challenge the forces of evil in order to create a World which affirms everyone's identity, rights and dignity.

Index